D0822953

TOUCHY
SUBJECTS

© 2014 by Craig Gross and David Dean

All rights reserved. No portion of this book may be repro-
duced, stored in a retrieval system, or transmitted in any
form or by any means—electronic, mechanical, photocopy,
recording, scanning, or other—except for brief quotations in
critical reviews or articles, without the prior written permis-
sion of the authors.

Library of Congress Cataloging-in-Publication Data

ISBN: 978-1497352001

Printed in the United States of America

www.craiggross.com
www.davidpdean.com

Cover and interior Design by: Ashton Owens
Editor: Adam Palmer

TALKING TO KIDS ABOUT **SEX, TECH,** AND
SOCIAL MEDIA IN A TOUCHSCREEN WORLD

|TOUCHY|
SUBJECTS|

CRAIG GROSS
creator of *X3watch, XXXchurch* and *iParent.TV*
with **DAVID DEAN**

This introductory part is important
—please don't skip it

We live in a touchscreen world. The more technology develops, the more integrated it becomes into our culture, the more it tends to involve some sort of screen. And, increasingly, that screen itself is becoming the way we interact with our tech.

So now the word touch is getting broader in its definition. We carry little computers in our pockets that we operate through touch. We use social media to share touching stories or reach out and touch base with someone virtually. And technology is opening all kinds of windows for a different kind of touch: sex.

These are all, in their unique way, touchy subjects.

And so the question becomes: how can we as parents guide our kids through responsible interactions with these touchy subjects? How can we teach them to use sex, technology, and social media in the best ways possible so that they can mature into responsible, emotionally healthy adults?

What's your approach, or do you even have one?

Maybe your son or daughter is young and you don't know when you should even broach a subject like sex or social media.

Maybe you're too nervous or embarrassed to bring up some of these touchy subjects in the first place.

Maybe you don't even realize how important these topics are.

Maybe you want to talk to your kids but just don't know what to say.

We wrote this book for you.

Who are we? We aren't medical doctors or academics with "Ph.D." written after our names. We're just a couple of dads who love our kids and who want to make sure they get the truth about touchy subjects.

As for me, I'm Craig Gross, and in 2002 I started a website started XXXchurch.com to help people overcome pornography addictions, whether they used it or made it. Over the course of that time, I've been called a "sexpert," I've been called "the porn pastor," and I've been called a number of other things that I'd rather not put in print.

I also helped to create iParent.TV in order to provide

a way for parents to stay on top of the turbulent and trend-driven world of technology so they can know what their kids are into, what they'll want to be into, and what sorts of restrictions they might want to put in place for touchy subjects.

I've traveled across the world talking to people—including many parents—about the relationship between sex, pornography, and technology. And while most parents are fine talking with me about this stuff, I've noticed that a lot of them are not comfortable talking truthfully with their kids about it. Whether it's from awkwardness or embarrassment or just plain not knowing what to say, most parents I talk to get uneasy when it comes to this topic.

Our different organizations are flooded with questions daily, and many, come from parents wondering exactly what to do when it comes to their kids and touchy subjects. They have tough questions, like:

- At what age do kids become curious about sex?

- My child said they saw porn at the neighbor's house. What do I do?

- My kid has gay friends; what should I say about that?

- I walked in on my son masturbating to porn, but my husband says this is normal. Is it?

- Should I expect my child to treat sex better than I did?

- I'm in the dark about popular apps; can you help me?

- What should I do about social media?

- I saw some inappropriate text messages on my child's phone; how should I confront them?

These are complicated questions that require answers, so my friend and colleague David Dean and I decided to take questions like these, along with other common questions about touchy subjects, and answer them through this book.

Whenever David wants to chime in, he'll do it after his initials so you can easily know what he has to say. Like this, for example:

DD: *Hi. I'm David.*

David is here because, as a full-time clean comedian, he's also traveled quite a bit and been able to use his humor to talk to parents and families about all kinds of touchy subjects in a frank but lighthearted way. Plus, while my kids are still relatively young (an 11-year-old boy and a 8-year-old girl at the time of this writing), David is a good decade older than me and has already lived through both his kids' adolescent trials and tribulations.

DD: Yes, I have. My wife, whom I call "Saint Betsy," and I have been married since 1988, and we have a 23-year-old son and a 20-year-old daughter. As they've grown up, we have had no problem in our family bringing up these issues of sex and technology and, as it's gotten more prevalent in recent years, social media: what to do, what not to do, where it goes, and when. And we started at an early age.

Sadly, in the rest of the world, our family is in the minority. Instead, a lot of parents treat these touchy subjects like hot potatoes. But guess what: whether you want to acknowledge it or not, these are issues you must address. Fortunately I've found, especially as someone who tells jokes for a living, that bringing humor and levity to the conversation makes it all the easier.

David and I met several years ago through speaking at different youth events. He was the comedy guy and I was the speaker/drama guy, and over the course of interacting with one another over several of these events, we struck up a friendship. Especially since I have younger kids while David has older kids; he's gone through some more things in his house than I've gone through, so I treasure his wisdom in those areas.

Working with XXXchurch.com has opened a lot of doors for me, especially when it comes to learning about the many different sides of human sexuality. I've worked with both pastors and porn stars. I've had conversations with everyone from the common man whose pornography addiction has spun out of control to the pornography actress whose substance abuse keeps her in front of the cameras.

As XXXchurch has grown, we've seen the need to educate parents on things beyond pornography and sex, on the types of touchy subjects that we've already mentioned here. The need has grown and the more I've interacted with others, the more experiences and insights I've gained that will be valuable when I have these conversations about touchy subjects with my kids.

Notice I used the word "conversations" just now. Plural. That was on purpose. Because talking about this stuff is not a one-time, get-it-all-out-on-the-table type of talk. This should be an ongoing conversation in your family, one you will pick up with your child again and again as they grow and mature. Think of it as a series of conversations that get progressively deeper.

David and I wrote this book as a couple of normal, average parents to help you have those ongoing conversations, in many parts, over the years. We've done it—so can you.

Because of the different stages of life we inhabit, as well as the different regions of the country (I'm in Los Angeles; David is in Indiana), we'll have slightly different answers to the questions we discuss, and this book is in no way intended to be comprehensive about all these different touchy subjects—there's just too much ground to cover. But we'll go over the basics and give you plenty of ideas to equip you as you begin to have these conversations with your kids.

Both David and I are involved in church-like activities, but this book is not about religion. It is about what we've seen with our own eyes, in our respective fields, and the conversation that must be active in your family. You have to get involved and stay involved, because, more than likely, your kids are already talking about some of this stuff with their friends. This book is meant to encourage you as you involve yourself in the conversation and guide your kids toward healthy thinking instead of forcing them to figure it out alongside their peers.

You don't even have to read this book all in one sitting. In fact, it's best if you don't. Read it as you need it—a question here, a question there; one principle now, another six months from now. As your children grow older, they'll continue to need advice. Think of this book as a resource or a type of manual. It's here to help you, not to embarrass you.

You may also notice we've split this book into two parts. The first features 28 bedrock principles that we feel strongly about. These are the foundations you need to understand before you initiate these conversation with your kids. We believe these principles provide the best approach to these (quite literal) touchy subjects. Read these first. Seriously, before you read any of the questions—or our answers to them—read these principles first.

The second part is made up of the types of questions parents have sent to XXXchurch.com and iParent.TV. Our answers may surprise you, and you may not always agree with everything we say, but I hope you'll at least hear us out and trust that we're coming from a place of honesty, with a sincere desire to help both you and your kids.

You can do this. You have to do this. You owe it to your kids to talk with them about these very important subject, just like you owe it to them to share your thoughts on religion, personal responsibility, finances, drugs and alcohol, or anything else you hold near and dear. If you feel embarrassed or awkward, you're just going to have to get over yourself and do it.

Do it for them.

Read on.

—Craig and David

March 2014

- Part 1 -

28 FOUNDATIONAL
principles for talking about
TOUCHY SUBJECTS

the earlier,
the better.

Talking about touchy subjects isn't like getting a driver's license—there's not a certain year requirement your child has to pass before you can say something to them about sex, social media, the perils of technology, or porn. There is no golden age, no perfect number of years your child must surpass in order to get their "I Now Know About Touchy Subjects" card.

You know your kids; you know your house. Feel it out. If you live on an isolated farm with no internet, no media, and no outside influences, then maybe you can wait until your kids are little older about these types of things.

But probably not.

Hopefully you're already having normal, regular conversations with your kids—about their lives, what books they like to read, what movies they like to watch, who their friends are... all those sorts of things that come with parenting. You should already be in their world and have an understanding of their maturity level. You should already have an idea what they can handle and what they can't.

As soon as you perceive they're ready to handle the basic information about the kinds of touchy subjects we're addressing in this book, you need to step up and start the conversation. Don't let the outside world beat you to the punch on this and potentially warp or distort the proper view of sex, technology, or even adulthood for your kids. They only get one chance to hear about anything for the first time—make sure you're the one giving them that input.

DD: As a comedian, I've been given a lot of opportunities to travel and speak to different groups of people about a lot of different topics, and of course, many of those topics are these touchy subjects. I've talked to men and to women. To married couples and parents. To college students, teenagers, and even middle-schoolers.

Let me just tell you: talking about sex can be awkward within any of those groups. But it's especially awkward among the middle-schoolers. I mention one thing about something like sex, and I get responses like, "Ooh, gross!"

"Sick!"

"Yucky!"

This is normal behavior. But even though your average middle-schooler might outwardly say something is gross, they're probably still intrigued at the genetic level. Kids are naturally curious about the world. They may not be

4

interested in learning anything at school, but they are
fascinated in learning about the world around them and
how it works.

They want to know what's up.

My son was no different—except he wanted to know
before he hit middle school. He was a very inquisitive
eight-year-old, so when he started asking questions at even
that early age, my wife and I knew the timing was perfect
to initiate these more difficult conversations.

He wasn't too young to wonder why we were
even bringing these topics up; he was at that perfectly
curious age, like all kids, full of wonder and amazement.
Their minds are sponges, ready to soak up any and all
information.

use everyday opportunities to talk.

This is actually just a good rule of thumb for parenting in general, but especially for talking about touchy subjects: incorporate what's going on around you in everyday life. Be aware of opportunities that present themselves to you or your kids, whether they're more subtle, like the announcement of a friend or relative's pregnancy (or your own!), or they smack you in the face, like stumbling into the middle of a gay pride parade (this actually happened to me and my kids—more on this story later). When it comes to having these conversations, you won't always have to revert to a textbook or manual—there are opportunities around you that you can talk about and relate with and to your kids.

Just keep your eyes open. You'll know when the time is right.

DD: *Nature fits this principle really well. Being outside watching animals interact presents many opportunities to either start a conversation about sex or continue one.*

At my house, we're big birdwatchers—we basically have an all-you-can-eat-buffet's worth of birdfeeders in our backyard in order to attract birds. We get a lot of cardinals, and we often see male and female cardinals coming to our birdfeeder in pairs to eat. Sometimes they even feed each other.

While our kids were still young, when we would see this kind of opportunity in nature, Saint Betsy and I would use it as one of many ways to discuss things like mating or marriage, pointing out the way these two cardinals would act as partners and care for each other. Then we'd help them connect the dots to see how that's the way we're supposed to mate.

I live in rural Indiana, and one thing we have out here is a lot of farmland. When you live on a farm, you get plenty of opportunities to get firsthand lessons from the animal kingdom on mating, sex, and reproduction. I personally didn't live the farm life growing up, but a lot of my friends did, and they found that just doing their chores was practically like an entire college-level semester in reproductive biology!

Looking for everyday opportunities like these is a great way to become more and more comfortable in having conversations with your kids. The opportunities are out there—you just have to watch for them.

too much,
too soon.

If you're like me, you want to have one talk about a touchy subject like social media or porn or tech, share all the details, go over everything, and then be done with it. Just get it out of the way in one swift motion and then never have to deal with it again.

But you and I both know better. These conversations can't look like that. Maybe that works for teaching your toddler how to use the Velcro strap on their shoes or your teenager the right way to start the lawnmower.

Talking about touchy subjects doesn't work that way. There are too many layers.

When you initiate the conversation, you only want to introduce that first layer. The basics. Then stop. You have their entire adolescence to go deeper, so just stick to the facts and don't give them too much information too soon.

So how soon is too soon? When David and I began putting this book together, we specifically chose not to break it down according to age. We have read several books along these lines, and I was surprised that so many of them did just that—simply turn to the section marked "Ages Seven Through Nine" and you'll find out exactly what to say to them about these kinds of touchy subjects.

Real life is not that easy.

Instead, you have to speak to your child's level of emotional maturity, starting when they're young and continuing all the way up to adulthood. Be mindful when you have these conversations that you're only educating them with what's necessary for that time and not giving them too much too soon.

DD: I do a lot of traveling, and I'll never forget the time I boarded a plane, stowed my carry-on, sat down, buckled up, and turned to the person next to me and said, "Hi, I'm David. Nice to meet you. I hope this flight goes well."

You know what happened next? Before we even took off, that person opened up their mouth and started sharing their entire life story with me. Every last detail of everything they'd ever done and said. Now, while I appreciate the sentiment (as well as the implication that I give off the vibe of being a person who can be trusted with such private information), I thought, Why are you telling me all this? Why now? What am I supposed to do with it? If I wrote this down, would I be transcribing your diary?

I was being given a story that should've been told at a deeper level of relationship, at a different time, and in a different setting. This was the kind of conversation I should be having with a good friend over a cup of coffee in my living room, and lasting deep into the night. Not with someone I just met while sitting on a puddle-jumper to Cleveland, nursing a tiny plastic cup of Dr. Pepper that's mostly just ice.

Unfortunately, as parents we can tend to do the same thing with our children. In just a few minutes we can unload years and years of wisdom that we've gathered about a topic to a child who isn't ready to hear it. Instead, give them what they need for that time and leave it at that.

write things down in advance

Preparation is a beautiful thing. It helps you get your thoughts focused. It helps you stay on track when that conversation wants to derail. Preparation is a major key to getting things done.

What I mean is: I want you to be prepared. Especially when you have an initial touchy subject conversation with your child, you'll probably have a tendency to share it all—to have the entire conversation in one sitting and get it over with (which is a bad thing; see Principle 3).

I can't stress this enough: talking about these things is not a one-time event; it's an ongoing conversation, and the way to avoid packing every bit of information you possess into one giant nuclear warhead of a conversation is by having a master plan. That way, when it comes time to start a conversation, you know exactly where you're going (and where you aren't) and you won't leave anything out (or put anything in that you don't mean to yet).

You don't have to write out a Shakespearean soliloquy that will enthrall and captivate your audience—a simple list of bullet points you want to cover will do. Just don't go into these conversations unprepared.

DD: I'd go so far as to say this: write three bullet points. Especially if you're the type of person who has difficulty thinking quickly on their feet, or if you're uncomfortable even having one of these conversations. Limiting yourself to three simple topics that you initially want to cover with your son or daughter is a great way to keep yourself on track.

Expect questions from your child, and if those questions cause the conversation to deviate into unexpected territory, then follow the conversation there (taking care not to give more information than is necessary). Your bullet points are there to help guide the conversation, but they aren't submarine missile launch codes that must be followed to the letter.

Honor your child's inquisitive nature. You have your main points written out, so you can always return to when the time is right. You, my friend, are prepared.

you and your spouse need to talk first.

This principle is for those of you who are married, and you shouldn't talk to your kids about touchy subjects until you've first talked to your husband or wife about how you're going to talk about them.

Over the last ten years, I've dealt with a lot of people who are used to keeping secrets, whether it's hiding their porn addiction or their Facebook affair or any number of other things. And often this leads to a mentality that says, "Well, I've misused sex or technology or relationships in the past, so I don't have any authority to speak about them in my kids' lives."

I've seen far too many parents use their past mistakes as an excuse not to talk to their kids. (Plus, it's a convenient way to feign humility and try to present a perfect past to their son or daughter.) They don't say anything and then their children have to figure it out for themselves, only to wind up making the same mistakes their parents did.

You want to avoid the line of thinking that says, "I have no authority to tell my kids what to do," and the best way to do that is to make sure you and your spouse are on the same page before you engage in a conversation with your kids. Don't let your husband or wife be caught off-guard and find out after the fact that you said something to your children they weren't aware of.

The best thing to do is to sit down and have a lengthy conversation with your spouse. Determine what you're going to say, how you'll handle any prospective questions your kids have, and how much detail you'll go into about your past.

And be prepared, because a conversation like this with your spouse very well could bring up a bunch of other issues like your past and your first experiences with sex. Maybe your spouse doesn't even know about your previous sex life, but it's important to get it out there. You and your spouse's collective past is going to shape the way you have this conversation with your kids, so you must be in agreement and lay it all out, talking openly about yourselves and your history—whatever it might hold.

DD: This would never happen, but let's say for the sake of argument that I'm hanging out at my house one day and I just happen to overhear my wife talking on the phone with a friend. It's their standard friendly chitchat, and then my wife says, "I just applied for a job today—I think it's going to be a really good fit. Probably the best job I've ever had, but I'll have to move to Canada to take it."

Now let's further suppose this is the first I've ever heard of this rather important and major news. Don't you think I would feel just the slightest bit betrayed? In marriage, you share all the major milestones together, from taking job opportunities to having children to buying your first house to shopping for hand soap for the guest bathroom.

Starting these important conversations about touchy subjects with your children are some of the biggest milestones you'll have with them. Shouldn't you start on the same page? Shouldn't you and your spouse get together and agree on what to say and when to say it? Shouldn't you approach this with as much unity as you would your careers or home life? It's always a good idea to keep the lines of communication opened in your marriage.

Along those lines, I get really bothered when I hear a great deal about topics like sex or porn from women and hardly anything ever from men. In the course of working with XXXchurch, I've noticed that men tend to not be interested in or involved with having these conversations with their kids.

Are you listening, men? It is your responsibility to

lead in this area. Hopefully you're leading in other areas at home already, but especially here. Don't pawn off these conversations with your son on your wife. Take the initiative and open the dialogue with your son. He'll thank you for it.

know what your kids are talking about.

I am fascinated by the number of parents who are clueless about the types of things their kids are involved in. We all want to hope and assume our kids are still the radiant, innocent angels they were when they were newborns, but this will get us nowhere. We must look at the world as it is, not as we want it to be, and part of that means we have to get into our kids' worlds and take an active interest in what they find interesting.

Admittedly, with technology today and the speed of communication, it's tough to be in the know about everything. Parents, you're at a disadvantage, especially if you aren't savvy about the internet or social networking. But you need to do the best you can to know what your kids are talking about when they talk to their peers.

I'm not saying you need to watch every television program they do, or read every text message they receive, or be with them nonstop. But you must get a pulse on where your kids are, what they're doing, who they're hanging out with, who their friends are—and not just their friends on social media. I'm talking about their real friends.

And when it comes to the computer or mobile device, know what your kids are doing when they go online. What apps are they using? What websites do they visit? How long do they stay? Who are their friends there? What are their conversations about? What are they watching, reading, saying?

What about their phone? How are they communicating while they're away from you? You already know how they talk when they're in your house—how do they talk to their friends, their teachers, other parents?

One last thing: don't think you can read some book (even this one!) or scour some website (even iParent.TV!) to learn everything kids are into these days. These types of things require you to engage in your kids' lives so you can know what's really going on. Not only will it help you in your conversations with your children, it will also help your relationship at the more basic level of simple connection.

DD: We have friends living in the Dominican Republic, and they often remark to us how they feel as if they exist in a completely different world. The economic situation is far from what they're used to in the United States, the cultural customs are strange, and everyone speaks a foreign language.

Sometimes talking to our kids can feel like a long-

term stay in some exotic land where we don't fit in, don't understand the language, and where the local customs make no logical sense. Walk with your teenager into any store in any mall and you'll enter a different world.

But as parents, it's important to stay connected to our kids and the world they're living in by seeing who they're engaging in conversation with and who they spend time with. Know your kids' friends. Meet them. Welcome them. Have them over for dinner so you get comfortable with them and they get comfortable with you.

When it comes to phones, I can only tell you what we did in our house. We always had a policy that, at any time, Betsy or I could pick up the kids' phones and look at their text messages. And in return, we let them do it with our phones. It was a great way not only to know what our kids were talking about, but also to show them a level of trust in the other direction.

This is also a great opportunity to let your personality shine. As a comedian, I take extra pleasure in deliberately embarrassing myself. So I like to connect with my daughter by incorporating some "hip lingo" and using it incorrectly.

For instance, I'll send her a text message that says

something like, "Do you want to have dinner? LOL."

Now, for those of you who don't know, "LOL" stands for "laughing out loud," and in the context of that text it makes no sense. But I use it as a humorous way to let my daughter know that I understand where she's coming from, that I want to get in her world and relate to her there.

And then she makes me watch Glee.

it's probably going to be difficult.

I'd love to tell you that talking with your kids about one of these touchy subjects is going to be simple and easy. No hassle, no mess. A few minutes and you're out the door.

It won't be like that.

It's going to be tough. Your kids may not want to hear some of these things, especially the ones related to sex. They may get freaked out that this information is coming from you. They may plug their ears with their fingers and dig their heels in against growing old. They may say things that upset, frustrate, or even hurt you. Don't let it deter you— have a conversation anyway.

Or, on the flip side, sometimes it can be difficult because they might have questions you won't be able to answer. Don't fake it—admit your ignorance and your willingness to seek out answers with them. They might have questions you don't want to answer. Do it anyway.

Yes, there are things in life that are hard—but they still must be done. We don't get to ignore or avoid things because we find them to be difficult.

Sometimes it's okay to change course in order to avoid hardship—like heading down a side street to avoid a traffic jam—but this isn't one of those times. And it's going to get progressively more difficult as your children grow and learn more, and are therefore able to comprehend more. Embrace the difficulty and you'll do better.

DD: *Here's a story about having embracing a difficult conversation. When my son and daughter were teenagers, I had Craig install the X3watch software on our computer at home. At the time, this was a program from XXXchurch. com that monitors everywhere you go online, and if you go anywhere it thinks might be questionable, it emails a report to a friend or an accountability partner (they have since developed it into a much more feature-rich program). Now, I'm not very technologically advanced, so I was glad that Craig took it upon himself to put the software on my computer, and then he took it a step farther and set himself up as the accountability partner.*

Time goes on and one morning I get a call from Craig. "David," he said, "I got your accountability report and there's porn all over your computer's browser history. What's going on?" Apparently, in the middle of the night earlier that week, our computer had been used to visit many adult websites.

I knew this wasn't from anything I'd done, and since it

happened during my son's junior year in high school, we naturally assumed he was the culprit. Betsy and I had to contemplate the difficulties of talking with him about this behavior—it's not really something you want to expose and discuss with your son.

Nevertheless, I went to him and talked to him about it, and he reassured me that it wasn't him. After a little digging, we came to the conclusion that it was instead my son's best friend, a young man who had spent the night at our house the same night as the activity showed by the report. After everyone had gone to bed, he'd gotten on our computer and violated the rules of our home.

Crisis averted! I called Craig back. "Craig, we're in the clear. It wasn't me and it wasn't my son—it was one of his friends."

"Great," he said. "But you know, this happened in your house, so you need to have a conversation with that kid."

I did not want to do that. I wanted to forget about it, push it under the rug, pretend it never happened, and hope the problem went away. But adult websites never go away, especially when you're a teenage boy. One look and they can suddenly become very addictive. I owed it to my son's friend to break through my own inhibitions and have a good talk with him.

For three days I wrestled with this until Betsy and I finally came to the conclusion that Craig was right and I needed to have a talk with our son's friend. I sat him down and he was repentant, ashamed, embarrassed, and broken. Fortunately, he was responsive, and this was ultimately a healthy, healing conversation that helped steer him away from the pitfalls of porn and toward a life-giving career.

Crisis averted again! I called Craig and told him I'd talked to this kid, and he said, "That's great that you confronted him, but he's still in high school. You have to talk to his parents, too."

No way. This boy's parents were good friends of ours, so that made it all the more difficult to consider sitting down with them and talking about it. Would they be defensive? Would this come between us and wreck our relationship? They didn't even know about my relationship with Craig, the "porn pastor," or that this software was on our computer. Would they feel like I'd set their son up to get caught?

There were so many variables and obstacles that made it difficult, but Betsy and I knew Craig was right—we had to talk to our friends about their son. This topic is dicey enough as it is talking about it within your own family, let alone talking to your kids' friends or your kids' friends' parents. But in the long run, you have to do it.

In our case, it wound up being a good conversation that helped alter this young man's life. Now he's living an honorable life and is a much better influence on our son.

It pays to make the difficult choice.

asking questions doesn't mean they're doing it.

Obviously, with this principle we're not necessarily talking about your eight-year-old. But as these conversations progress throughout the teenage years, your son or daughter is going to have more and more questions about some of these touchy subjects, maybe even some crazy ones.

Who knows where these questions come from? They may have heard other kids talking at school, or they may have gotten it from a movie or something they saw online, or they may be asking something that sprang into their very creative, fertile, adolescent minds. Don't assume the worst and think they're asking from experience.

This is a very important principle, because you want your son or daughter to know that you're a safe place for asking questions. When they want to know something about a touchy subject, where do you want them to turn: to Google or to you? Google doesn't get on their case for seeking information, and you shouldn't either. If you jump down their throat for asking a simple question, what's the likelihood that they'll ask you another one?

Instead, respond lovingly when they bring up something out of the ordinary. Reassure them that you are safe and that you're glad they came to you. Answer honestly and calmly to guide them to the truth. All will be well.

DD: The fact that your kids are asking you in the first place is a huge compliment to you and your parenting skills. When your child comes to you and says, "Mom, Dad, I saw this on TV" or "some friends at school were talking about this" or "I read this online" and asks for your take? That's huge.

Answering questions creates a fantastic opportunity to enter into a dialogue with your children about these very important topics, so don't let any question scare you. No matter what the question, take it all in stride. A friend of mine encourages parents in his realm of influence to be shocked on the inside and calm on the outside. Radiate calmness.

Imagine that your child comes to you and asks, "How many times can you have sex in a day?" Now, that's a pretty shocking question, because, as a parent, you'll tend to leap to the assumption that your child is doing nothing all day but having sex! But the fact of the matter is, you don't know where that question came from, and if you yell at them for bringing it up, they're probably never going to ask you about sex again.

They'll still want answers, though, and since you've yelled at them and assured them you aren't a safe place, they'll turn to their friends. Or worse, the internet. Is that really where you want them to get answers about sex?

Be calm. Stay calm. Don't assume.

when it comes to sex, talk with them about reasons to wait.

David and I agree that waiting to have sex until after you're married is the best way to live your life. But we also believe it's not enough just to tell kids what to do or what not to do and never explain the reasons behind those rules. It's not enough to say to your kids, "Don't have sex," and then follow their inevitable questioning with, "Because I said so."

Instead, you have to talk with them about legitimate reasons to wait, whether they're spiritual reasons, health reasons, or any other reasons you may consider.

So what are some reasons to wait? Here are just a few:

- You don't risk disease.

- You don't risk pregnancy.

- You won't experience the heartbreak that comes with being compared to someone else.

- You won't have the heavy emotional baggage that sex brings with it, meaning you're less likely to be depressed or moody.

- You'll make your eventual spouse feel unique and loved all the more.

And those are just the tip of the iceberg.

The point is: there are plenty of reasons to wait, and you should let your kids know those reasons, so they understand why they should wait to have sex. When you do that, you are providing them with a reason to buy into the philosophy and internalize it, making it a stronger ethic that will help them resist any temptations they may encounter.

DD: We put this principle into action in our family one day when we went shopping for a car. We pulled onto the lot at the dealership, and immediately there was a brand new car sitting on the lot, shining in the sun and looking crisp and new. A little further down were about six "pre-owned" cars, looking their best but still plainly used: the body styles were older, the paint wasn't as fresh-looking, the bumpers had little chips and dings, and the interiors were starting to go threadbare and smelled like an attic in the summer.

I made a point of showing the differences between the new car and the used cars to my children. Once I had them drooling with a Pavlovian response over that new-car smell, I said, "Which would you rather have?" And of course, they both picked the new car.

It became a perfect analogy to talk about marriage, and how, on the day you marry, you want a spouse who is like that new car, physically and sexually. You want to be the only driver, so to speak.

And so, it would make sense, that if that's the kind of person you want to get married to, then you should also be that person for your eventual husband or wife. So the idea of waiting until marriage becomes not just a parental preference but a sensible act of love for the person you eventually will spend the rest of your life with. That's a much better reason to wait than an oversimplified "Don't."

be honest.

Sometimes clichés are clichés because they're true, and even though we've heard them a million times, they haven't lost the essence that caused them to be created in the first place. In this case, one particular cliché couldn't be more true: honesty is the best policy.

Don't make things up. If your child asks you a question and you don't know the answer, admit to your ignorance.

Maybe you have stuff in your past that you aren't proud of or did some things that you don't want to admit. Maybe you're afraid your kids are going to ask you about your youth and you won't like the answers you'll have to give.

It doesn't matter. Be honest.

DD: Kids are often far smarter and intuitive than we give them credit for, and they know when they're being patronized or when someone's trying to sell them something. If anyone can sniff out whether you're being totally forthcoming, it's your own child. So be completely honest.

Use your past history as a way of teaching them. If you made mistakes, let them know those mistakes and the lessons your learned from them. Be sure to tell them you learned those lessons the hard way, and talk about any regrets you may have.

If you feel good about the way you handled sex during your adolescence, talk to them about the way that feels as an adult and the sense of accomplishment and satisfaction you have.

Regardless, whatever they ask you, look them in the eye and tell them the truth.

And if they ask you a question you can't answer, be honest about that. Tell them you don't know, but you'll find out and get back to them. It will be a great way to continue the conversation.

talk about fighting peer pressure.

As your children get older, they are going to get the message from their surrounding world—whether it's friends, acquaintances, or just our culture—that everyone is doing something and so, consequently, they should be, too.

Don't wait for them to face this type of thinking on their own—be preemptive and talk to them about it. Prepare them for it. Let them know that they probably will come to a point where they'll have to stand up for what they believe in, for what you have taught them. Yes, they may know people whose behavior is on the wrong side of these touchy subjects, but that doesn't necessarily mean it's okay, nor does it mean it's allowed.

I have a niece who is twelve years old at the time of this writing, and she has convinced her parents that she needs to be on Facebook. Now, Facebook currently has a policy that says you have to be at least thirteen in order to use their website. This policy has a reason to exist, because Facebook doesn't want just anyone to be able to jump on and start handing out status updates. So as part of the process when you sign up for an account, you have to enter your birthday. If you're under the age of thirteen, Facebook will deny you any use of the site.

The only way to get an account for a person under thirteen? Lie.

First of all, I wouldn't really want any thirteen-year-old on any social media; I would rather have them involved with their real friends in face-to-face communication. But there is so much cultural pressure right now to participate in social media, even at a young age. It is the thing to do, the thing to have. I've talked with many parents who don't really want their kids on Facebook, Twitter, Instagram, and the like—who don't even have children old enough to use it those sites or apps—but who cave in and let their kids lie about their age in order to get an account because, well, that's what everyone else is doing.

Don't buckle as a parent to what our culture or what our society is saying to your children. Instead, teach your kids that there are reasons behind the rules and that they can and will have to stand up for their beliefs. It's perfectly acceptable to challenge the culture and say that some things are not okay.

DD: This is one of the reasons we emphasize talking to your children about touchy subjects at an early age, rather than waiting until they're in their teens. In all the time I've spent talking with students, traveling all over the country, I have discovered that all too often, the biggest influence a teenager has in their lives—the voice with the most credibility—is the voice of their peers. By talking to your kids at an early age, you are able to talk to them at a time before that peer-shaped voice takes precedent, when, instead, you are definitely the biggest voice in their lives.

Establish at an early age that you are your child's biggest fan, that you support them, and that you believe in them. Let them know early and often how much you care for them, that you are a safe place for them, and that you want to be the biggest influence they have in their lives. You'll be preparing them not just for adolescence, but for the rest of life.

don't avoid the 'safe sex' talk.

As we mentioned in Principle 9, our preference is to tell our kids to wait; unfortunately, that usually gets expressed simply as, "Don't have sex." And while that's what I would recommend for my kids, it doesn't mean that's what is actually going to play out in their lives.

While the idea of safe sex is pretty acceptable within our culture, there has long been a huge debate in church circles about whether we should even be talking about it. There are fears that just bringing up the topic of safe sex is going to lead to rampant sexual activity amongst even our most chaste young ones.

But let's face the facts: talking to your kids about condoms or birth control does not mean you're approving of sexual activity, any more than talking to them about car insurance means you're giving them free rein to get in a wreck.

Listen, I hope my kids wait until they're married to have sex. But if they don't, I hope to God they at least have safe sex. And if that's the case, I don't want them to learn (or not learn) about safe sex from the person they're about to have sex with. Or a friend. Or really just anyone other than me.

This is a fine line, because you don't want to give even tacit approval to your child to have sex. You have to be clear about what you believe and what you expect from them. But you have to talk to them about what safe sex truly is, otherwise you are not preparing them for every possible temptation they may face.

Temper this conversation with plenty of reminders of reasons to wait (see Principle 9), but with a mindful attitude about the realities of temptation. In the end, you just want to give your child as much information as possible so they can make the best choices for their lives.

DD: Speaking of birth control: my daughter has friends that are actually on the pill, and not so much as a means of birth control but because it helps control their moods, makes their menstrual flow more regular, and even helps with their complexion. These girls aren't even sexually active, but they know about birth control. Your daughter might need to know, too.

don't assume your kid is perfect.

"My kid would never do that."

Trusting our child's judgment is a common perception we have as parents. We want to believe that, when push comes to shove, they're going to make the right decisions. However—and I hate to break this to you—that kind of thinking is often wrong. The fact is, you don't know. You aren't with them all the time, so you can't assume your kid is perfect.

DD: When my son entered preschool, Saint Betsy and I went to a sort of opening day ceremony to kick off his academic career. All the parents gathered and the different teachers said a few words of introduction to help us get to know them and to set expectations for the upcoming school year.

When the time came for our son's preschool teacher to speak to all the parents, she said something wonderful and inspirational that I've never forgotten: "We won't believe everything about you if you won't believe everything about us."

Kids don't always get it right. They're going to say things at school about us as parents that might astonish us—because they aren't true. They're going to say things at home about their teachers that might sound incredible—also not true.

And we saw this borne out with our children—they would tell as story that would make us scratch our heads, and then, the next day we would show up at school to find that the actual story was completely different, and that their teacher had actually given them graham crackers, not grams of crack as originally reported.

Get all the facts first before you assume your child did or said something, or didn't do or say. And realize that they make mistakes, same as you.

share your values.

I've seen a lot of parents be very involved in sharing values with their kids as they're young. I've also seen a lot of those parents, for some reason, stop instilling those values as their kids get older. It's easy when kids are young— whatever you say, they tend to believe. But the older they get, the less they take your word for it.

My kids are still young, so they take what I say as fact, and they'll even recite it back to their friends to settle disagreements or just to wow them with some bit of information. It's the same way with interests and hobbies. My kids wind up getting interested in a lot of the things I'm interested in, especially my son. I played soccer and so he wants to play soccer. I like music and going to concerts and, what do you know, he does, too.

When your kids are young, imparting your values to them is easy, so you do it, hoping that they'll take those values on with them into their adolescence and adulthood. That isn't always the case, though, and hoping isn't enough. Don't ever stop sharing your beliefs, your values, your moral compass, your thoughts. They may act like they aren't listening to you, but somewhere, deep down maybe, they are. And it means a lot to them.

Trust me on this one.

DD: *While I was growing up, my dad was a fairly quiet guy while my mother was more assertive and tended to be "the voice" in the house. Still, I can remember times when my dad and I would be in town on errands, or on vacation, or just out somewhere, and seeing his reaction when a beautiful woman walked by.*

Kids look to their parents for cues on the ways they should behave, so whenever this happened, I would always look at my dad to see what he would do. And you know what? He never gave any of these women a second glance. He would recognize them, maybe say "hello," and go about his business. No leering looks, no ogling.

I still treasure that about him to this day.

Through subtle ways like that, my dad taught me that women are not objects, they are people, created by God, who deserve to be loved and respected. Now, fortunately, my dad was able to communicate that to me in a nonverbal way—but not all values can be shared like that. It's best to share what you believe openly and honestly through dialogue and discussion, and then to back that viewpoint up through the way you act in real life.

Your kids are watching. What are you sharing?

patience.

You will be put to the test and challenged as you have these conversations. Really, this applies to all of parenthood, but especially when it comes to talking with your kids about sex. And because of all those tests and challenges, you have to develop a deep sense of patience.

Don't say too much at once—be patient and trust that the right times will come to impart as much information as your children need.

Don't get angry—be patient and trust that whatever questions you're being asked or whatever comments your child is making are coming from a good, honest place.

Don't lose sight of the big picture—be patient and trust that tempering yourself for the long run will pay off.

Patience is a virtue, and if you need patience, your children will give you many opportunities to develop it.

DD: When talking to your kids about sex, you're presenting an issue that they are more than likely not very familiar with. Yes, they may have heard tall tales from their friends or gleaned information from television and movies, but as far as sex as a whole goes, they're clueless.

Most children tend to be very inquisitive, especially the younger they are. When you have these conversations with your kids, you're going to get asked a lot of questions, and oftentimes you will probably be asked the same question over and over, just rephrased differently.

In these instances, you have to be willing to sit and listen, to talk with them calmly and encouragingly. Some kids may absorb this information, process it, and be done with it relatively few questions.

These kids are rare.

Instead, be prepared for the more likely instance: that you will have to be patient with your kids as they process this very critical component of existence.

**accurate
information.**

Since David and I are just average, everyday dads and not experts, we spent a lot of time reading a lot of different books on these topics in preparation for writing this one. Some of them were stuffy, while others were even stuffier. And in doing all that reading, we realized something: while all of them recommend the principle of giving your children accurate information, there's a difference between being perfectly accurate and generally accurate.

We want to encourage you to be honest and share the truth, but we're granting you a little leeway here when it comes to naming certain body parts, physical conditions, possible temptations. We would recommend that you be accurate without being stuffy or textbook, as if you're handing this stuff down to your kids from on high. You want to relate to them, so be accurate in the general information you give while still personalizing it for their ears.

It's also important to be relatable without being cavalier. You don't want to come across as making light of these touchy subjects or treating any of them disrespectfully. Emphasize the wonder and delight and sanctity of these subjects without making them seem like homework.

DD: This idea of accuracy also applies with theological truth. If you're going to share truths on touchy subjects, make sure you do it accurately, and be prepared for additional theological questions while you're at it. You may have to explain why, say, it was okay for Jacob to have four different wives while these days we try to stick to just one. You never know. Kids think of these things.

listen.

This one might wind up applying more to dads than to moms, because dads tend to talk more and listen less while moms tend to do the opposite. So that's the first thing: don't be the one doing all the talking.

However, listening doesn't stop when your conversations are over. Yes, you want to listen in that context, but don't let it end there. I know I keep saying this, but it's important to remember—talking with your kids about touchy subjects isn't just one trip for ice cream where you say all you have to say and are done with it. No, this is an ongoing conversation you'll have with your kids throughout their adolescence and into adulthood.

Which means you'll have multiple opportunities to listen.

And even then, don't stop listening. Listen to them when you're not even specifically talking about these topics. Listen to the ways they talk to their friends or to other adults. Keep your ears open around your kids, and you'll be amazed at what you'll learn. And if your kids bring up sex or porn or technology to you, be all ears. Don't take that as a cue to start sermonizing or delivering a master's-level lecture series— instead, sit down, be quiet, and listen to what they're saying.

DD: *A very wise person once said that God gave us two ears and one mouth so that we can listen twice as much as we speak. As you can imagine, since I am a professional comedian and person who talks for a living, this means I am obligated to do a lot of listening.*

This could not be truer to us parents. We must pay attention to what our child is saying.

And this doesn't apply only to the words that come out of your children's mouths, either. Our kids communicate with us in a lot of nonverbal ways, through the faces they make, their posture, the way they walk... the list goes on. As parents, we must be attuned to those methods of communication as well. We need to listen to their emotions, to their physical expressions. They're always communicating—are you always listening?

if you
don't know
the answer,
admit it.

We've already covered this in part in Principle 10, but here we want to take it the next level. You already know not to make stuff up, and that saying "I don't know" will not discredit your authority, nor will it make your children question everything you say. On the contrary, being honest about any lack of knowledge you have will make you more relatable to them. So if they ask a question and you don't know the answer, then be honest with them and tell them that.

And then you need to go one step farther: promise to provide an answer and then deliver on that promise. This is one of those parenting principles that applies across the board, but, once again, especially in the realm of touchy subjects. Admit your ignorance, but deliver an answer to them as quickly as you can. If you have to stay up all night doing research, do it. Give your kids the answers they want and deserve.

DD: I started the conversations about touchy subjects with my son when he was eight years old. Saint Betsy and I had already agreed that we needed to start the conversation specifically about sex sooner rather than later, and we'd already talked amongst ourselves about what that would look like. Then an opportunity came when he and I were coming home from a camp in northern Wisconsin, in the middle of a lengthy drive. The time felt right to start talking about it, so I made it happen.

It was an open dialogue, and I shared with him the basics of how a man and a woman join together in the wonderful, God-created act of sex. And as I'm explaining this, he's taking it all in with eyes bigger than silver dollars. He didn't ask a whole lot of questions right then, but he was definitely intrigued by it.

The next day I took him to a Chicago Cubs game at Wrigley Field, and as we entered the gate, we saw a man in a wheelchair pushing himself up a ramp and into the stadium. My son stopped me, discreetly pointed to the man, and said, "Dad, can he do it?"

"Do what?" I said.

He leaned up to me and whispered, "Have sex."

And in that moment, I had to be honest and say, "I don't know." There are times where that is a perfectly appropriate thing to say, and this was definitely one of those times. Because I didn't know whether this man's sexual organs were affected by whatever affected his legs.

I suppose we could've asked the man, but that would have been a little awkward. He was just trying to enjoy himself at the ballpark, and since he was a Cubs fan, he didn't need the embarrassment of my eight-year-old son asking about his sexual proclivities. The team on the field was embarrassing enough.

(Full disclosure: I am a lifelong Cubs fan. I am used to disappointment.)

By the way, in this case, I wasn't able to promise an answer, so the mystery of whether this particular man in a wheelchair could be sexually active will go unsolved. Somehow, my son made it through adolescence without ever possessing that knowledge.

don't hide your past.

Your past is your story. You can't change it, but you can own it. Maybe you even went through a situation or acted in a way you're still trying to figure out. Regardless, by owning up to your past, you have the opportunity to speak into your kids' lives in ways you never imagined. Your story gives you a platform and it gives you the authority and wisdom of experience.

I can see this unfolding even in my own marriage. My wife and I have different pasts and different upbringings, and throughout our adolescence we treated the various touchy subjects in different ways. In the right time, we'll share our respective stories—and the lessons we learned from them—with our kids. It's just part of our lives, and therefore a part of their history.

Whatever your story is, when the time presents itself to do so organically, share it with your kids. Don't assume they're going to follow in your footsteps either way, but use your story. If there are things you would do differently, share those. If there are times you felt like you got it right, share that. You owe it to them.

This principle is one you'll have to come back to time and time again as you have these conversations with your

grace.

kids. Now, obviously, as a parent, there will be times when you will have to punish your children or let them reap the difficult consequences of their wrongful actions. That's just part of the territory. You'll have to figure out what types of consequences your kids will have when they engage in activity you disapprove of.

But ultimately, there's grace. The only way you'll be able to continue to have these conversations in your house, to continue to provide an environment where your kids feel comfortable having these conversations, is through continual grace. When you extend grace in the proper way, you're showing your kids that they are safe with you, and that they can continue to come back to you time and again with their questions, comments, stories… whatever.

What if you think your children don't deserve grace? Too bad. You don't either. None of us do.

That's why we give grace—because we need it.

DD: Grace is often simply offering forgiveness to those who don't necessarily deserve it. And when you offer it, your kids are watching you do it. When you extend grace to a friend, a family member, a coworker, your child will see that and, hopefully, emulate it. Because at one time or another, we're all in need of some grace. We give it because we want to get it.

reassure them that not everyone is doing it.

"But Mom, everyone is on Facebook."

"Dad, everyone texts during class."

"But everyone is having sex."

Any of these sound familiar? Kids seem to be genetically predisposed to seeing things in terms of "everyone" and "no one."

I remember when I was fifteen years old, dating my first girlfriend, and I was just excited to be able to kiss her. One day I was talking about this girl with a friend of mine, and he said, "Man, she doesn't want you just to kiss her. She wants you to bang her!"

Intrigued at this newfound terminology, I said, "What does that mean?"

He explained it to me. My response was, "Wait, I'm fifteen and she wants me to do what?"

I talked to a couple of my other friends that explained to me what "banging" was and told me "Everyone was doing it."

Now, fortunately, I had enough foresight to recognize that, even if it was true that "everyone" was doing it, that didn't make it okay for me.

Let's look at it this way: roughly half the marriages in the United States today end in divorce. So, in some respects, we can say, "Everyone is getting a divorce." Does that make it okay? Does that mean we should all just give up, stop fighting for our marriages, stop working together as husbands and wives, and just head to divorce court?

What's wrong with being in the minority? You can sidestep the fallacious argument that "Everyone is doing it" with this: so what? Who cares? You don't even have to poke holes in the everyone-is-doing-it lie. Instead, remind your children that there's nothing wrong with going against the tides of culture, especially if you believe your way is better.

Teach your kids to stand up for what they believe in and not just follow the crowds.

DD: *The media tends to play a big role in this, especially in shaping the values of our kids and teenagers. Watch your average movie or television show, read your average young-adult novel, take even a cursory glance at the internet, and it sure does seem like "everyone is doing it." The message to kids is this: your entire generation is doing this stuff, and if you aren't, then you're abnormal.*

That's what our culture would like for your kids to believe. Do they? Have your kids bought the lie, or are you helping them understand that they can rise up against that cultural tide and deny the argument? Are you showing them that the media distorts things? That their peers aren't always being completely honest?

use real-life situations to talk about touchy subjects.

One evening I was watching TV with my kids—maybe it was American Idol or the Grammy Awards or something— and the musician Bruno Mars showed up as a guest star. He performed a then-new song called "The Lazy Song." I thought it was a catchy tune, so I downloaded the single from iTunes and gave it a few more listens, enjoying the production and the melody without paying too close attention to the lyrics.

That was my mistake, because the song has a lyric that says something about "meeting a nice girl and having some really nice sex." And I'm listening to this with my then five- and eight-year-old kids, who are pretty great at picking up song lyrics quickly!

Unfortunately, I hadn't realized the lyrics said anything like that until I heard my children singing it.

Now my oldest already knew what sex was, so I used my lyrical mistake as an opportunity to talk to him about what my wife and I believe about sex, that it's something really special and unique, and so you shouldn't just go meet a girl and have sex like in the song. Fortunately, he got it right away.

With my youngest, things were a little thornier. She didn't know what sex was yet, and wasn't really ready to hear all about it, so I just said, "Hey, let's not use that word, and when you're older, your mom and I will talk to you about the reasons why."

In both cases, I was able to seize an opportunity that presented itself to have a conversation about a very touchy subject with each of my kids, one that was age-appropriate and emotionally stable.

And then I deleted that song from my iPod.

DD: This is where being aware of your surroundings and your child's media intake comes in so handy. When you're conscious of their world and are aware of what they're watching, what they're listening to, what the culture is telling them, you have much greater ability to seize opportunities like that.

Even better—now that we're in the age of the DVR, you can even pause a television show right then and there to talk about what you're watching.

My daughter enjoys watching some shows that provide very little entertainment value (to me, at least), but lots of opportunities to have conversations. A show like, say, 16 and Pregnant provides a means for me to talk to my seventeen-year-old daughter about the very real possibilities that come with adulthood, especially that of having a baby. Thanks to the conversations that show has spawned between us, my daughter sees it as a cautionary tale, not just a form of entertainment.

Now, as a parent, you're responsible for setting the parameters in your home of what's okay and what isn't. Your parameters may be different from mine or from David's. But you have to understand that those parameters are not always going to be in place, because your kids are not hearing about this stuff only at home.

My son took an acting class a few summers ago, just a little weeklong day camp. Every day when we dropped him off, there was a sign-in sheet with a different, fun question for each day, things like "What's your favorite thing to eat?" or "Who's your favorite actor?"

Everyone in the class were between the ages of seven and ten, and one day the question was "What's your favorite TV show?" I dropped off my son a little late, so almost all the kids had filled in their answer. I happened to scan the list momentarily and saw titles you would expect from a bunch of kids: Hannah Montana, Spongebob Squarepants, that sort of stuff. But mixed in there I saw titles like The L Word, Dexter, Modern Family, and Keeping Up with the Kardashians.

Fortunately, on the way home, I was able to use this as a way to talk to my son about what is and isn't appropriate viewing for kids his age.

One more thing to consider: if it's inappropriate for your kids, does that make it inappropriate for you? Sometimes yes, sometimes no. Everyone has to answer that question in their own way—but regardless how you answer it, please consider it and think through your answer so that you can at least be intentional in the way you treat your own media consumption.

talk about it again and again.

We live in a world where people like to get things quickly. I wanted to get back into exercising, so I tried P90X, which is a workout regimen you do for 90 days. It gets pretty brutal, and within 15 days I was toast and gave up. But the whole program speaks to that idea of doing something—in this case, getting fit—super-fast.

This is everywhere in our world. Drive-through windows, iPhone apps, crash diets, self-checkout lines... we are bombarded with convenience that can often achieve great results.

These conversations you're having with your kids about touchy subjects? They don't work like that.

It's going to be tough, it's going to take time, it's going to last for years. In my house, I want to talk about these things both as a family and individually with my kids. I envision at times that my wife and I will talk to one of our kids together, or my son will go to my wife while my daughter comes to me, and vice versa. We are in this for the long haul.

We're dedicated to making our house a place where no question is off-limits. There is no such thing as "out of bounds" when it comes to the inquisitiveness of my children.

And this becomes even more important as my kids begin

to bring friends over to the house—I'm not going to apologize for having these conversations with my kids' friends any more than I would at having them with my own children. If something comes up, I'm going to address it, whether that kid's parents are having a conversation with them or not. If someone is downloading crazy apps over my internet connection or bringing over inappropriate video games or using our computer for porn, you better believe I'm going to talk to that kid about touchy subjects.

DD: A lot of parents tend to treat this talk as a one-time, one-off situation. "Look, I read the book and the expert told me what to say, when to say it, how to say it, and now that that's over I can breathe a huge sigh of relief."

No.

Are you tired of hearing that yet? Have you gotten the message?

It isn't over. This is an open dialogue, an ongoing process, and a line of communication that must always remain open with your child. And this is really just a great pattern to develop for life: the idea of remaining open and working at revisiting these things again and again, not *just with your children but also with your spouse. Because honestly, we all need to be reminded of the truth every now and then.*

initiate.

More than likely, the first conversations you have with your kids are only going to happen if you initiate them. As they get older, hopefully they will bring their questions to you, but for starters, the initiation is all on you. So do what it takes to get the conversational ball rolling.

This can be tough, especially for those of you who may never have initiated anything with your kids. Plus, it's hard to know when to initiate that first conversation, especially if you've been putting it off for too long.

If my parents ever had a conversation about any of these touchy subjects with me, I don't remember it. I was on my own. But much later on in their lives, they adopted my brother, and, once again, had the opportunity to initiate the conversation.

My brother was 13 and I was 35 when I went to visit them in northern California, and I saw a book on my dad's nightstand called *What's Going on Down There?* It's an illustrated guide to help parents talk to their kids about sex and puberty and some of the things we're talking about here. Now, I'm sure this book is great for younger kids, or a boy who has just started to enter puberty. But when it comes to a 13-year-old young man who already weighed 200 pounds and was six feet tall? Probably not going to cut it.

I started tracing the history of this book in my parents'
house and found out my mom had bought it a long while
ago and told my dad he should probably go over it with
my younger brother. Instead of initiating the conversation,
though, my dad put it on his nightstand, where it sat,
gathering dust for Lord knows how long.

And guess what? My brother already knew what was
"going on down there." My parents had really missed an
opportunity. Don't do the same thing with your kids.

*DD: The summer of 1998 was the summer of the home
run chase, when sluggers Mark McGwire and Sammy Sosa
were going back and forth to see who could hit the most
home runs in a single season of major league baseball.
Now, unlike Craig, who seems to think that soccer is a sport
worth following, I am a huge baseball fan, and so is my son.
That summer, we were in constant contact about the home
run chase. I'd go out on the road to do shows and ministry,
but we would stay in communication and give each other
the latest updates on the chase.*

We did this literally every day. We were both so excited

to be sharing these father-son moments about who hit home runs that day, who didn't, who was in the lead, who we predicted would come out on top, and which of these phenomenal athletes we were rooting for.

It lasted all summer long, and as September rolled around it dawned on me: I'm having these great conversations with my son about who is going to be the home run king, and I'm glad it's me and not anyone else. There was no other father figure in his life sharing this incredible, epic adventure with him.

And that realization led me to a deeper epiphany: if talking with my son about baseball was so important to me, how much more important should talking about touchy subjects be? I don't want anyone else having those important conversations with him, any more than I wanted him sharing excited conversations about the home run title with anyone else. Believe it or not, the home run chase was a major influence on the way I talked with my son about many different things.

ask
questions.

Just as much as you need to be open to having your children ask you questions, you also need to ask them some questions yourself. As your kids get older, they're going to be embarrassed, and they may not want to answer you when you ask questions, and they may even say something like, "Dad, Mom: stop." You have an opportunity to set the standard for your conversations by asking questions from the very beginning.

Take, for example, the first conversation I had about sex with my son. When I prepared for that, I made sure to have my ideas together in my head (I didn't take my iPad out there, with slides and graphics) so I knew where to start. And the first thing I said was, "Son, do you know what sex is?" Instead of starting with a long, drawn-out impartation of all my knowledge and wisdom, I started with a question.

He gave me a smirk that I'll never forget. That look told me that I was starting right on time and that asking that particular question was the right thing to do. Now, I'm a pastor, and I'm running in all the right circles and my kids are in charter schools, but that smirk said so much.

"What?" I said. "What are you smiling about?"

"Dad," he said, "my friend said this girl in our class is

sexy." And then he just kind of smiled some more.

"Do you know what that means?"

"No."

His smirk had told me that he'd heard the word enough to know it meant something, but that he was in the dark about it. That simple little question kick-started what is becoming a lifelong conversation between me and my son, and I'm confident it will lead to more and more questions, in a back-and-forth dialogue that lasts for years.

DD: So many parents don't do this. I've seen parent after parent after parent approach touchy subjects from a high-and-mighty stance, thinking they will be the only voice in the house when it comes to these kinds of topics. They delude themselves into thinking That's Just How It's Going To Be.

But the healthiest kids aren't the ones living under a dictatorial relationship with their parents. Instead, they feel free to come and ask questions. And how will they get to the point where they feel that freedom? By answering questions you ask.

And it's important to remember to keep asking

questions as your kids get older. Don't wait for them to come to you with questions, though they certainly will. If it's been awhile since they've talked to you about sex, take the initiative to ask if they have anything on their mind. It's a great way to keep the doors of communication open.

have a sense of humor.

Touchy subjects are usually pretty serious topics, and these are serious conversations that can easily wind up feeling tense and awkward. How can you combat that? Use humor.

In the same way that you want to look for everyday opportunities to talk about touchy subjects, you also want to be on the lookout for ways to slip some humor in to put your child at ease. Be smart about it: if you're making a strong point, don't undercut it with a joke. But if you see an opportunity to work some sort of witticism into your conversation, by all means do. Don't be afraid to laugh a little.

DD: Humor disarms. Whether it's in a marriage, in a family, or in a parent-child relationship—humor is the great disarmer. Laughter defuses a lot of bombs, and levity is good. I promise you I'm telling the truth, and I'm not just saying this as a professional comedian.

Sometimes when you're having a talk about touchy subjects with your kids—especially the sex-related ones—they might start giggling and laughing as a release mechanism. They aren't being disrespectful—they might just feel nervous or awkward. Don't chastise them for it—join in with them! Recognize their discomfort by laughing along,

and you'll strengthen the bond you have them.

One more thing: you have to make sure you use humor appropriately. Laugh at the situation; not at your kids. Never use humor to undermine or demean your children and never make jokes at their expense. Laugh with your kids, not at them.

remind your kids that what they want to do with their bodies is their choice and nobody else's.

I hope my kids are leaders and not followers. I hope they stand their ground when it comes to decision-making and won't be persuaded by someone else to do something they don't want to do, especially if it means giving up something so valuable as their sexuality or their innocence. What they do with their body must be their choice.

It is imperative to impart this power to our kids. Your kids must know that they do not have to allow someone to talk them into doing something they don't want to do. They must know that their life is the sum total of the choices they make, and that no one can make those choices for them.

Help them choose wisely.

DD: When it comes down to it, this is a self-esteem issue. When you reinforce to your children that their body is a temple and is something to be respected, adored, and loved, you are building their self-esteem and reminding them about the importance of the choices they make.

You must also be sure your kids know that you are a safe place for them if someone else has abused them in any way or forced them into submission like rape or sexual abuse. Because this type of abuse is so personal and has such a weight of shame associated with it, kids (and adults, too) often don't tell anyone about it until years after the fact. You have to let your kids understand that you care about them and that they can trust you with their hurts. And if your child has been abused, you must report it the authorities.

talk to
your kids
specifically
and
individually.

If this is possible, it's better for dads. Sometimes, with some touchy subjects, it's better for dads to talk with their sons or for moms talk with their daughters. There are others that might be best received by a daughter talking with her dad or a son talking with his mother. For example, my wife will probably talk someday with my son about relating emotionally with women and what effect a man's actions and words can have on a woman's emotions.

Don't assume that every facet of these conversations works the same way or needs to be discussed by the same people. Treat each topic as its own thing, and talk about it in the way you feel is best to discuss that particular topic.

There might even be things that you talk about as a family. This is great, as long as you don't try to just lump everyone in together. Tailor everything to your child's specific needs.

DD: Men, when you take your sons aside; moms, when you take your daughters aside—look them in the eye and talk to them. By the time they're adults, you should have spent so much time looking them in the eyes that you could detail their irises to a police sketch artist.

Talk to them. Listen to them. And in so doing, you will

be creating wonderful memories in their minds of all the times they talked with their mom or dad and learned about this wonderful creation called sex.

- Part 2 -

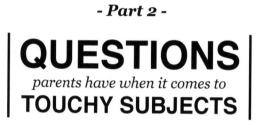

QUESTIONS
parents have when it comes to
TOUCHY SUBJECTS

One summer I was invited to speak at a large gathering of about 35,000 kids. That's a lot of kids, so in order to make sure they got to experience the whole conference, the organizers split them into several different groups and offered several different breakout sessions they could attend.

I headed one of these breakout sessions, and I decided to call it "Questions You Can't Ask Your Mama About Sex." I wrote a book with Mike Foster called *"Questions You Can't Ask Your Mama"* you can get on Amazon. When I walked into the room for my first session, I was shocked. The room seated about 7,500, and it was packed out. Either these kids were really interested in me as a speaker, or they were all huge fans of the band that opened up the session, or—most likely—they were all there because of the topic.

When it comes to touchy subjects, kids have questions. They want to know.

Here's how I set up the session itself: I put a phone number on the screen and invited the kids in attendance to text their questions to it—any and all questions they had on the topic of sex—and told them I would do my best to answer those questions.

I did three of these sessions, each one 90 minutes

long, and over the course of those sessions, I fielded 1,300 questions—so many that the program I was using to receive texts got overwhelmed and I had to upgrade my data plan!

Kids want honest answers.

Kids *deserve* honest answers.

Over the last several years, as we've worked at XXXchurch and iParent.TV with so many different people, both kids and adults, we've discovered something: while kids have questions, and adults who are struggling with sexual addictions have questions, parents have questions, too. Maybe more than kids.

The remainder of this book consists of the types of questions we get from parents. Now, neither David nor I is pretending to have all the answers to every possible question, but we do have experience in fielding these kinds of questions and providing honest answers, responses that work in the real world as we see it. Hopefully you'll be able to use these answers over the next several years of raising your kids.

In writing this book, we've attempted to order the questions in rough categories so you can find the ones most pressing to you at this particular stage of your child's life. We have intentionally kept our answers applicable to all ages, trusting that, as your child's parent, you will know when the time is right to tackle the next topic.

We've also divided the questions up into seven different categories. They are:

1. Sex

2. Puberty/Masturbation

3. Pornography

4. Relationships

5. Culture

6. Online

7. Sexting

Hopefully that will help you find the question (and answer) you're looking for more quickly.

DD: *I happened to be speaking at the same conference Craig mentioned at the beginning of this introduction, but I didn't get my own breakout session. Since I wasn't speaking at the time of Craig's session, I decided to attend and sit in* the room as he did his thing. It was fascinating—every time Craig put a new question up on the screen, the kids would applaud and cheer, excited about the question itself and its forthcoming answer.

In the back of my mind, though, I began to ponder how these types of questions should be answered by parents, not a complete stranger. While I was glad these kids could get the information they wanted from someone like Craig, I was saddened that they would rather ask these questions at a conference in front of thousands and thousands of their peers instead of going home and asking their parents in private.

Hopefully this book will help you coax these questions out of your kids. Our hope is that we will provide you with information and the desire to have these conversations in your home so your kids don't feel they have to get them from a stranger—even one as nice as Craig Gross.

Oh, and my favorite question of those three sessions? "Why are boobies so awesome?" I may have been the only adult present who gave that one a standing ovation.

Anyway, on with the questions...

|QUESTIONS ABOUT SEX|

Do I really need to talk with my kids about sex? Isn't the word "sex" a dirty word?

Obviously, since we wrote this book, we would answer this question with an overwhelming "yes." You must have this conversation with your kids. Don't allow someone else the privilege of introducing them to such an integral part of life—this is something you need to do for your child, and you need to do it as soon as you feel they are ready to begin.

Give them information in doses over time. This is not a one-time talk; this is a lifetime conversation you'll have with your kids.

And when you talk to them, let them know up front that the word "sex" isn't a "dirty" word—it's a wonderful word that describes a marvelous gift and a great thing. So many times, we miss the boat and guide our kids' behavior by telling them not to do something, providing them with lists of rules and boundaries, but with no context and without explaining why.

I've seen these types of prohibitions backfire, not just among adolescents but also among the recently married. I have acquaintances who were told their whole lives that sex was bad and wrong, and once married, approach it with a negative stigma. Instead of being a glorious gift and physical representation of the unity of soul, sex in their minds is a "dirty" thing that should be avoided—because that's how they've always thought of it. They just don't know how to have fun and do it the way God intended.

Instead, talk about sex as a wonderful thing that is worth waiting for. Speak positively of it. Help your kids understand the reasoning behind any prohibitions you place on it. This will go a long way toward helping them develop a proper mindset toward sex.

DD: In his autobiography, shock-rock singer Marilyn Manson wrote something along the lines of: "If you don't raise your teenagers, I will gladly do it for you." Your kids are going to hear about sex eventually—that is not the question. The question is, are they going to hear about it from you?

My mindset is this: sex is a topic that is near and dear to my heart, and I want to make sure my kids get the true story about it rather than some distorted view presented to them by a media figure or their peers.

Any good thing can be taken out of context, manipulated, and distorted until it looks like a bad thing. Every generation amplifies itself and has a tendency to take something that is good and pure, then distort it until it becomes "dirty," and that's what our generation has largely done with sex.

A lot of parents become afraid to address the topic of sex with their kids out of fear that it's become taboo and something you don't talk about. Especially with the pendulum swinging the opposite way in our culture, where sex is becoming more and more ubiquitous and permissive. The knee-jerk reaction for some parents then is to try to distance themselves from it, leading you to think that talking about sex at all is "too worldly."

This is backward thinking. Your kids are going to hear about sex one way or the other, and if you want them to hear about it being used correctly, you'd better make sure you approach it the same way.

At what age do kids become curious about sex?

There is no such thing as a golden age when kids become curious about sex, any more than there's a golden age when they get their first tooth or walk on their own or become toilet-trained. These things just happen when they happen along your child's particular developmental path.

So when should you start talking to your kids about sex? Should you wait until they ask? Should you wait until they show outward signs of entering puberty? Should you wait until the morning of their wedding day?

While there is no magic age of understanding, we can give you some ballpark ages where you can initiate conversations with your kids about sex. Personally, I think somewhere between ages seven and eight. If your child gets to nine years old and doesn't know a thing about sex yet, you're probably waiting too long, because it's more than likely that other people are starting to talk to them about it already.

Talk to your kids about sex when you think they're old enough to handle the basics. And don't short-change them— kids are smarter than you think. I had the talk with my son when he was eight years old, but it was brought about by some behavior that I saw in him and some ways he reacted to what he was seeing in the media. I knew the time was right and pounced on it.

On the other hand, if your kids are already asking you about sex, then stop avoiding the inevitable. You owe it to them to give them an honest explanation, regardless of their age. We can argue and debate all day long on whether that's too young or not, or we can seize the opportunity that's being presented to us as parents.

There are a lot of factors that go into the questions our kids ask us. I don't know their influences: your home, your background, the culture of your family, where your kids go to school, what media you let them consume, what media they consume on their own... the list goes on. But if your child is asking you about it, they've already been exposed to the topic and now it's up to you to grasp the bull by the horns and give them the honesty they deserve.

Times have changed, and you can't just assume that the way you learned about sex is the same way your kids should learn about it. Maybe your parents waited until you were a lot older; maybe they didn't say anything. It doesn't matter. If your kids are asking, you need to answer them.

DD: *I would even go farther than Craig and say start having these conversations with your kids when they're between the ages of five and six, especially if they're boys. Boys are very aware at an early age of their penis and they create and invent many uses for it. They want to know whether this thing sticking out of their body does more than just pee, and inherently they know it does.*

Six, seven, eight years old—that's around the time you can start talking with your kids. And if your seven- or eight-year-old is coming to you and asking about sex, that raises a red flag. To me, that says they've been introduced to the concept somehow, most likely in an unhealthy way, or that they've been given information on it, which was most likely wrong information they heard from someone at school or saw on some movie or television show.

This makes it a great opportunity for you to jump in and clarify their wrong or misinformed notions. It isn't a prison sentence—it's an opening to help them see how sex really works and how it really should be used.

I live in rural Indiana, where many of our friends live on working farms and ranches. Talking about sex is very common for them, as they're constantly around animals reproducing and giving birth. They use that as a natural segue to talk about sex; there's no need for you to reinvent the wheel.

If you have even a remote amount of creativity or imagination, you'll be able to weave discussions about sex into your everyday conversations. Look no farther than nature, or emotional instances, or even things like hunger— all of those are legitimate openings to talk about sex.

Finally, these ages aren't set in stone, even within your own family. It's up to me and my wife, as parents, to treat our different kids as individuals and talk with them whenever we sense the appropriate timing.

Watch your kids. Listen to them. Pay attention. You'll see signs of curiosity eventually, and once you do, it's only a short step from there to talking with them about sex. When the time is right, you'll know.

What is the most important thing about sex to tell my kids?

It is extremely difficult to narrow the topic of sex down to just one thing, because there are so many other things wrapped up in it. It isn't just about physical expression — there are emotional, psychological, and even spiritual components to sex that can't be covered in just one talk or boiled down to a single "most important thing."

That said, if there is only one thing I want my kids to know, it would be this: sex is a great and wonderful creation of God. It isn't dirty, it isn't wrong. It isn't gross, it isn't sick. It isn't bad, disgusting, evil, or something to be avoided.

Sex is a gift.

The great thing about initiating these conversations with your kids is that it gives you the opportunity to frame sex in this way, where you discuss it as a marvelous gift that serves a specific, yet multi-faceted, purpose. Yes, sex perpetuates the human race by leading to children, but it also brings husbands and wives closer together and keeps those marriage bonds strong. It has its place and its own parameters. It opens the door for you to say, "If you want to experience sex in the best way, then here are the guidelines."

Have you ever been to Ikea? If not, it's a giant home

furnishings store that originated in Sweden before expanding to quite a few locations in the United States. They have very modern-looking furniture at affordable prices, which makes it great for people like me who want to be stylish without spending a ton of money.

But while I love furniture from Ikea, I really hate putting it together. Because Ikea is an international company, they intentionally use no words in their instructions—it's just a series of cryptic cartoons depicting a guy with a smiling face magically assembling furniture with a screwdriver.

These directions are useless to me.

In fact, my wife and I have probably had more arguments about assembling Ikea furniture than we have about anything else in our marriage. We'll have, say, a desk that comes in four separate boxes, and instead of using Ikea's instructions, I'll just try to figure it out, putting it together every possible wrong way. I'll put a drawer in backwards, or put the desktop on upside-down, or put the right leg where the left leg should be—I really know how to mess these things up.

And then, once it's messed up, I don't want to have to go through the trouble of redoing it, so I'll just leave it halfway assembled in the hopes that it will spontaneously rearrange itself into its proper shape at some undetermined point in the future. Maybe the smiling cartoon man will come by with his screwdriver and fix everything.

My wife, on the other hand, will tell me how wrong I'm being. She'll grab the Ikea bible—that little comic book they try to pass off as assembly instructions—and will walk through it step by step, undoing my bad workmanship and doing the job exactly as Ikea recommends.

There's nothing wrong with the furniture or with the instructions—the problem comes when I try to do things my own way with a complete disregard for the way it was intended to be done.

That's what I want to share with my kids. That sex is great and wonderful in its time and within its designed purpose. I want them to know that, when they try to put it together on their own, they're going to fail and wind up frustrated and emotionally broken. Sex is a simple act that goes together even easier than Ikea furniture, but its complications go far, far deeper, which is why we must treasure it for the gift it is.

That's what I want my kids to know.

DD: *To me, sex is a lot like the game Twister. Remember that game? It's a big mat you lay on the floor with all these giant, colored dots on it. Someone spins a spinner that determines whether you will put your right foot, left foot, right hand, or left hand down, and which color of dot you must use. Eventually you get pretty contorted, and the last person to fall down wins. When there are multiple players, this leads to a big tangle of arms and legs, and, generally a whole lot of laughter when everyone falls down.*

Sex is a lot like that. There'll be limbs going in every direction. There will be sweat. There will be grunts. There's really no winner or loser; it's just a bunch of fun.

And then you want to play again.

Unlike Twister, however, sex works best when you do it with a person you're madly in love with and committed to for the rest of your life. It isn't a free-for-all and it isn't casual.

But when you do it the right way, it's a game you never want to stop playing.

How in-depth should we be about sex with our children at each age?

In the midst of writing this book, our family car hit the 60,000-mile mark. To celebrate this milestone, my wife went to the glove compartment, pulled out the owner's manual, flipped to the "Maintenance" section, and found a long list of scheduled maintenance items we needed to have done in order to keep our car running at peak performance. The car manufacturer, through rigorous testing and uniformity, knows exactly when these types of things need to occur and conveniently spells it out for you in the manual.

You're probably getting tired of reading this by now, but we'll say it again: this book is not like the owner's manual for your car, where you can just flip to the index, find the entry that says "Routine maintenance for age nine," and go from there. There is no checklist for thirteen that lets you know it's time to replace the timing belt.

As your kids age, you will be able to introduce them to more and more concepts and realities about sex, and while you'll have to determine those things for yourself, you know you can start with the basics: Boys have a penis, girls have a vagina. One goes into the other and that's how babies get made. That's called "sex."

When I told this to my son, he said, "That's gross."

"No," I said, "it's a wonderful gift. And it feels really good."

He thought this over and said, "Well, do you do it every night?"

That's the plan, I thought. But what I said was, "Not usually."

But that was it. That's all the ground we covered. I didn't get into other means of sexual gratification, or masturbation, or different positions, or anything of that nature. Just the facts. That's all he needed to know at the time, and as he grows older, I'll relay more information to him.

DD: I look at it as being like a dad talking with his son about sports. When your child is young, you introduce them to the games themselves: baseball, football, basketball, soccer—you name it. And as they get older, you start to talk to them about the intricacies of the game, the situational stuff, the quirks in the rulebook. The infield fly rule or the "tuck" rule.

If your child decides to play that sport, you work with them over time to develop their game. One summer you may help them develop their free-throw shooting. Another year you'll teach them about defense. Another year later and you're showing them ball-handling skills and the pick-and-roll. Every year, as they develop a foundation, you teach them a little more to build onto that foundation.

Sex is the same way. It's an ongoing conversation where you continue to deepen their understanding and build on what they've learned. As their bodies develop and change, you give them more things to think about along those lines, pointing out along the way the emotional and physical changes they'll go through.

But unlike sports, when you have sex the right way, everyone wins.

Both my kids are in soccer, and I'm a coach for their teams. I've noticed as they've grown older that, while they have more responsibility on the field, my responsibilities as a coach increase as well—for each age level they attain, I have to add to my training in order to be certified as a coach.

When my daughter was currently in the "under-five" group, which is really just a beginner's category for kids who are starting out and are just learning the game. And the fascinating thing is: at this age, it doesn't even matter which goal they score on. The league just wants to teach the kids to kick the ball into the goal, temporarily ignoring the different sides that exist in a normal soccer game.

During one game, my daughter scored four or five times—all on the other team's goal. One of the parents on our team was getting livid with her and started yelling at her that she was going the wrong way. My wife is usually the kinder of the two of us, but she wasn't going to have that. She turned around and said, "You don't know what you're talking about! It doesn't matter at this age!"

Right now, all my daughter needs to know is: score. Next year, should my daughter continue taking soccer, she will learn that there is a difference between which goal you should score in, and we'll be able to add to the foundation of knowledge she received all last year when she was allowed to score at will.

Talk to your children at a level they'll understand, then increase their information incrementally as they grow older.

What should I say when my child asks where babies come from?

My wife and I have told our kids from the time they were able to comprehend that God made them. That's the foundational truth. But when my wife was pregnant with our daughter, our son could plainly see that mom's belly was growing because, as we told him, there was a baby in there.

At the time he was only about two or three years old, so when he asked us how the baby got in there, we just told him that God put it there. Because that's an honest answer that works for a three-year-old.

But once I had the first sex talk with him, I was able to do some explaining and help him connect the dots. I finished the talk by saying, "That's how we made a baby."

While sex and babies go hand-in-hand in the real world, they don't necessarily do it in your kids' minds. So when they ask you where babies come from, you don't need to get nervous and start worrying that your kids are sex-obsessed. They're just being curious. Be as honest as you can and use language they'll comprehend.

DD: *My sister and brother-in-law have a two-year-old* *daughter. Recently they were over at my house, and my* *niece was sitting on her mom's lap, poking at her stomach.* *Then she looked up at my sister and said, "Mommy, did I* *live in there?"*

"Yes," my sister said. "That's where you were for nine *months until you came out."*

Even at two years old, the curiosity of "Where did *I come from?" had arisen within my niece. Because it's* *natural! We all want to know that—it's part of our sense* *of identity. We innately have the questions of who we* *are, where did we come from, how did we get here—that* *curiosity is an innate characteristic. We would do well to* *honor it in our kids.*

How do I explain what is good or bad touch?

This is the perfect example of the type of conversation you want to have with your child earlier rather than later. My wife and I told our kids, at very young ages, what their private areas are—and we did this long before we told them anything about sex. We would take the opportunity while they were in the bathtub or even while we were changing their diaper to let them know, "This is your private area, it is off-limits, and no one is allowed to touch you here."

If you want, you can take this a little further and tell your kids that bad touch is any touch they don't want. Their body belongs to them, and they have the right to tell anyone to stop touching them, even if it isn't in a private area. If that person won't stop, then your child has the right to get away from them. Any touch that makes them feel weird or "yucky" on the inside is bad touch.

This doesn't have to be a big, drawn-out production; just a simple affirmation of what is right and what is wrong, which you back up in real life should the need arise.

DD: I have a friend who is an Indiana State Trooper, and he often speaks at elementary schools on this very topic. Why does he do it? Because it is so common in our society for children to trust adults to the point where they can be manipulated and taken advantage of. Most sexual abuse of children is not from strangers—it's from people they know, like a relative or friend.

Many times, once my friend has finished his talk, he'll have kids approach him and say, "This has happened to me." It happens more than you think, but kids place so much confidence and trust in adults that they rarely take the initiative on their own to step forward and tell someone else what happened to them.

It's okay to talk about this with your kids, and it's okay to ask them if it's ever happened to them. Don't be afraid of the answers. If you discover your child has been abused, seek out the proper authorities immediately. Don't ignore it and don't hope it goes away—your child has been violated and now they're looking at you to protect and rescue them. Do it.

My son thinks his penis is a toy like a guitar—is this okay?

This is normal behavior, depending on how old your son is. If he's, say, between the ages of five and seven years old, this type of curiosity is pretty standard. If he's thirteen, that's a whole different story. You also have to consider where he's exhibiting this behavior. If you're at home, that's one thing; if you're in a restaurant, that's something else.

Now, whether you want to allow this type of play is entirely up to you and the type of home you strive to have. You may decide some things are okay but other are off-limits—that's fine. But whatever you do, don't degrade your son if you happen to catch him using his penis as a rocket ship. You want to let him know that area is private, but not that it is dirty or something to be ashamed of.

Our ten-year-old walked in on us having sex. What do we do?

I'll have to answer this question by first asking one of my own: in the moment where your son or daughter walked in on you, what did you do? Did you yell at them to get out? Did you take a break to take care of them? Did you act embarrassed?

This happened to a friend of mine, and the first words out of his daughter's mouth were a horrified, "What are you doing to Mom?" He and his wife couldn't help but laugh and then gently remove the daughter from the situation. And of course, when he told me this story, my first response was: "Lock your door!"

These types of experiences are largely avoidable with a simple lock and a little bit of discretion. But while I don't want my kids to walk into the room during it, I do want them to know my wife and I have sex. As a youngster, I was always grossed out at the thought of my parents having sex, and I don't want that for my kids. I want them to understand the loving nature of sex and the necessity of it for maintaining healthy intimacy.

Should it happen to you, though, my only advice would be not to overreact. Remain as calm as you can, usher them from the room, and put a lock on your door for next time. If you don't have a lock, wedging a chair under the doorknob works just fine.

DD: My family has a very small house where you can hear just about everything that goes on, whether doors are open or not. This was a great way to keep tabs on our kids, especially during their adolescence, but it made it difficult for my wife and I to really find some privacy.

At night, there are a lot of fans running in our house. Noisy ones.

Even in the winter.

We had our share of close scrapes before my kids were ten years old. "Dad, why are you and Mom on top of the dryer?" Those types of things. It takes some creativity and you have to think on your feet (well, first you have to physically get on your feet), but we could always find excuses to get through those times.

Once when I was in high school, I walked in on my own parents having sex, and I was actually worried that my dad was beating my mom, especially because of the way he reacted when I walked in. It wasn't until years later that I put two and two together and realized he'd just been on the road for a long time and needed some time alone with his wife.

I'm a single mom. How should I talk to my son about sex?

I feel for your situation, and it certainly isn't an easy one. If dad's not around, not in the picture, not involved in your son's life at all, then yes, it is your responsibility to talk to him about sex. As uncomfortable as it might be, you can either avoid it (which will most likely lead to trouble) or embrace it (which will help steer your son down the right road). Be open and be as honest as you can.

Does your son have a father figure at all in his life? An uncle, a grandfather, a teacher, a coach, a youth pastor, a mentor at church? If so, seek out ways to involve them in the conversation. Ask them for pointers or whether they want to come alongside you in guiding your son's thoughts and perceptions on this all-important topic. Be proactive, and do it out of love for your son.

QUESTIONS ABOUT PUBERTY & MASTERBATION

My son/daughter has noticed that their body looks different from ours. When do I tell them about puberty?

Puberty is as much a part of life as growing up, and eventually your kids will have to go through it. Your son will start to need deodorant. Your daughter will need a bra and start shaving her legs.

The best way to have this conversation is father to son, mother to daughter. And, of course, the different stages of your child's development will happen at different ages, so there's no way to give an exact answer. However, as a parent, you want to get there before any of these changes start to happen in your son or daughter—you don't want him to think he wet the bed or her to think she's inexplicably bleeding to death one day.

These changes will occur, but you don't necessarily need to go into detail about them when your children are young. You don't need to be embarrassed or to embarrass them; a simple, "It'll happen sometime when you get older" will suffice.

Obviously, David and I are both men and fathers, so we've never experienced the changes that daughters go through on their way from childhood to womanhood. Both of us travel quite a bit speaking at different churches, and occasionally we take our kids with us so we can spend time with them.

David would trade off taking his son and his daughter with him, and my wife and I used to always kid with him that his daughter was going to start her period while she was away with him out of town. Man, was he terrified of that happening.

DD: Fortunately, that particular milestone happened while my daughter was at home with her mother for the weekend. But Saint Betsy had already addressed it with our daughter when she was a young girl, preparing her, letting her know her body would change and that she would eventually experience menstruation.

Children are full of awe and wonder and curiosity. It's truly one of the great joys of having kids that you get to experience that curiosity and guide it. But children often ask the questions that adults only think about but don't ask. "Why does that stick out?" "Why does that look like that?" "Why does that man only have four fingers?" "Why are you wearing an eyepatch?"

There is no inhibition and no filter—they ask what's on their mind. That's all they're doing when they ask these types of questions; they're just being curious.

One time, when my son was a young boy, we were showering after swimming at the YMCA, and there happened to be an older gentlemen in the shower stall next to ours, and he happened to be missing part of his arm. My son was staring a hole through the guy, not just at his casual nudity but also at his amputated arm.

As you might imagine, he had a thousand questions on the way home, all of which had to do with why this man looked so different from other people my son had seen. That was not the opportunity I was expecting, but I took it anyway and ran with it.

Puberty is a natural part of life, and more and more, it's happening at a younger age. And girls are smart—they can put two and two together more quickly than boys. Girls look at their private area and innately want to know what it does, how it works, why it works that way—they want the whole story. Boys look down and say, "Neat! A missile!"

Do I need to explain periods, pads, and tampons?

Whether you have girls or boys, they're going to hear about this stuff through their peers, so it becomes important to talk about these topics to make sure your kids have the right story. As I travel and speak at camps and conferences, I meet so many young women who have never had these conversations with their parents, because it's "too embarrassing." As a result, they're trying to figure out what's going on with them by asking their friends or just waiting it out. Is that really the way you want your daughter to enter into womanhood?

It even helps to explain to your boys that girls are going to be going through changes, and why, and what they can expect. You'll be helping them go a long way toward forming good, healthy relationships with the young women in their lives.

DD: I was about eleven or twelve years old, prepubescent, when one day, quite by accident, I walked

into the bathroom and stumbled upon my aunt, who was
a teenager at the time, switching out her tampon (or, as
we wound up calling it in my house, "changing the plug").
Terrified, my eyes got wide and my jaw fell open. Not
satisfied that I was scarred enough, my aunt decided to
make it worse by explaining it to me.

I've never been so shell-shocked in my life. I didn't
know what she was talking about, didn't want to know
what she was talking about, and just felt uncomfortable all
around. She had the best of intentions in trying to help my
understanding, but it was just so extremely awkward.

If only my parents had had the forethought to explain
to me that our bodies change, and this is how a young girl
becomes a woman. Oftentimes, that's all a boy needs to know.

And he certainly doesn't need to see it acted out for him
by his aunt.

Do I explain to my kids what orgasms or semen are?

Yes. These are things that are either implied or talked
about in many TV shows and movies, so, once again,
your kids are going to hear about them. If your son has
masturbated even once, he's experienced both of these, and

he deserves to know what they are, what their purpose is, and how to handle them at his age.

Believe it or not, I've dealt with many people through XXXchurch.com who grew up so sheltered by embarrassed parents that they went into marriage not knowing what an orgasm was and not understanding the purpose of semen. I've known many married couples where the wife has never experienced an orgasm during sex and doesn't think anything is wrong with that. And this all goes back to the way their parents handled these topics—or didn't handle them, really—when they were younger.

You owe it to your kids to talk about these things, but at the right time. You probably won't bring up orgasms in your first sex talk, but you will eventually. I've had a sex talk with my son, but he isn't ready for this level yet. I'll know when that time approaches, and I'll talk to him about it openly and honestly.

DD: I'm not above using euphemisms for these types of conversations. If your younger child has a lot of questions when you're talking to them, it's okay to say, "It feels really good to mommy and daddy," instead of saying,

"You have an orgasm." Instead of describing the process of insemination, you can call it "seed" or describe it "like a fish swimming in a stream."

The time will eventually arrive when you can introduce your kids to the actual terms for these things, but for the younger child, your focus needs to be more on aiding their understanding of the process than of getting the terms perfectly correct. After all, they aren't going to be taking a written exam on the topic (unless they go to a really weird school!).

I noticed that my kid's sheets are wet (either because of a wet dream or masturbation). What do I do?

My parents never talked to me about wet dreams, so I was scared to death when it first happened to me. I didn't know this was something uncontrollable, and I didn't know that it happens to every guy. After my initial exposure, I talked to some friends about it and was finally able to figure out what was going on, but the fact remains that I shouldn't have had to. And neither should your son.

Instead, let your son know that this may, and probably will, happen to him eventually. It doesn't usually happen at opportune times, but it happens to every male on this planet, and your son is no exception.

Do I talk to my kids about masturbation?

The long and short of our answer is that you must talk to your kids about masturbation. This is not optional— it's mandatory.

I first heard about masturbation in seventh grade, and I heard about it from my youth pastor. Now, believe me, by that point, I'd already figured it out. I just didn't know it had a name, and I didn't know whether it was considered good or bad. I had my suspicions, but I wasn't entirely sure. My youth pastor wound up answering some questions I had, but, sadly my formal introduction to the topic came after I'd already discovered it.

When I first talked to my son about sex, he thought it sounded gross. When I told him it felt good, he responded with, "Yeah. It kinda tickles." He had realized even then that, when he's playing air guitar, it didn't hurt him. He's not old enough or far enough along in his physical development to know yet that it can feel really good.

Most kids are introduced to masturbation innocently enough. There's no real understanding of sex or of simulating it—there's just an understanding that, hey, this feels good. It kinda tickles.

But these days, pornography's rampant accessibility has changed the game. Porn is now inextricably linked to masturbation, creating a pattern and a habit that is very tough to break. I deal with people almost every day who get so addicted to porn and masturbation that they would rather simulate sex with themselves than have the real thing with their spouse.

Don't get fooled into the line of thinking that says masturbation is a way to prepare yourself for having sex. Masturbation is easy and requires no one but yourself, so it's not a way of preparing for sex or getting ready for it. Not at all. Sure, there's a climax, just like sex, but the emotional and relational components of sex—the things that make it so rewarding—are missing. There's just you, and that's unsatisfying.

You need to talk about masturbation with your kids before the sheets get stained, before the towels get scrunched together and hard as a rock. Again, prepare them with knowledge beforehand so they don't have to figure things out on their own.

DD: If your sixteen-year-old son claims he has allergies and is going through four boxes of Kleenex a day, he isn't just sneezing in his room. Without a doubt, it is inevitable... your teenage son is going to do this. The chances are even good that your teenage daughter is going to do this. It's probably going to happen more often with boys, but both boys and girls are going to wind up experimenting with masturbation. Once they find out their bodies are capable of this, that such extreme pleasure can be found so easily— literally at their fingertips—they're going to find all manner of reasons to stay home and try it.

Masturbation can take over your kid's life. It can interrupt their performance at school, it can hamper their relationships, it can intrude on their social life. Should you see these things happening, you should be aware that they could be getting addicted to it.

Masturbation is a powerful drug. I once met a man who was so addicted to it that he put his penis into a subwoofer and turned it up so loud that he blew out the speaker. He would use electric toothbrushes, electric massagers... anything he could to heighten the sense of pleasure. He would be in the shower and his mother would wonder where the Vaseline was.

I couldn't believe his mom was being so clueless. She washed his sheets. She washed his underwear. He had to have been stained beyond belief. God forbid his parents should run a black light in his room—what kind of craziness would they find?

This is a guy whose parents needed to talk to him about masturbation.

Masturbation can very easily become something you can't stop. It can start innocently enough—a simple longing for a natural pleasure—but it gets taken over with lust, with an uncontrollable longing, with a distorted thought life. At that point, it's dangerous.

During the course of my work, I've become friends with a man who is arguably the most recognizable porn actor in the world, Ron Jeremy. Ron is very famous in the industry because he is a well-endowed individual, and so one day I asked him, "When did you figure out that you can not only masturbate but also give yourself oral sex?"

"Oh, when I was a teenager," he said, "I realized it was long enough to put in my mouth."

Let me just tell you: by the time your son is fifteen, he's either thought about this or tried it. For most people it won't work, but it worked for Ron Jeremy.

And you know what Ron's father told him, upon learning about this behavior? "Don't worry, son. By the time you're eighteen, girls will do that for you." And now his son is the most recognizable porn star in the world.

Be careful what you say to your kids—you have no idea how you're influencing them. If you know your kids are masturbating and that pornography is involved in it, you owe it to them to have a serious conversation, because they are ruining their future sex life. And if you don't know what to say, go to XXXchurch.com and look for the resources we have to help you talk with your kids about this topic.

I caught my daughter touching herself. Any advice?

We're living in a day and age where an open conversation about this topic needs to happen with your girls, maybe even around the same time that it happens with your boys. You don't want to embarrass her or make her feel insecure or small, but you do want to address the issue head-on.

I'm all for joking around, but making light of serious topics, especially around or to your kids, will prohibit them from wanting to come to you when they find themselves struggling with these things. They'll be afraid that you'll make fun of them or won't take the problem seriously. If you embarrass them, even jokingly, and they say, "Oh, Dad, stop it," that's a sign that you need to let it go.

So in this instance, where you discover that your daughter is engaging in masturbation, it's a good idea for starters to let mom handle the conversation. Explain what's going on, why it feels good, and the intended purposes for those feelings. Your kids are going to be curious about those types of things, so fill them in and help them understand the bigger story.

DD: Kids are very aware of their bodies and are innately curious. They want to know what's going on with themselves and aren't afraid to experiment and find out what their bodies are and are not capable of, so it just makes sense that they're going to discover masturbation. If you can guide them through this particular minefield, you'll be helping them greatly.

Those feelings of sexual pleasure exist to connect intense pleasure with a moment of intimate bonding between a husband and wife. The pleasure of an orgasm is more than just a climax—it's the climactic moment of a story that husbands and wives tell together each time they have sex. It carries emotional power and isn't something to wield lightly.

| QUESTIONS ABOUT PORN |

I walked in on my son masturbating to porn, but my husband says it's normal. Is it?

This goes back to a foundational element of parenting, which is that mom and dad have to be on the same page. When it comes to sex and what counts as "normal," this is a lot easier to agree upon when your son is seven than when he's a teenager. But regardless of your children's age, you and your spouse have to be in unity about how you're going to handle these types of situations.

Be aware that your kids will play you against each other in order to get what they want. They are smart and perceptive, and if they know that mom and dad aren't on the same page, they will use that to their advantage. I'm not suggesting that your kids are manipulative or devious; I'm simply acknowledging this fact of human behavior.

Now that we have that out of the way, I'm really hoping this husband will call me, because I can let him know that letting your son masturbate to porn is not okay and should never be considered "normal" behavior. I don't care if you grew up flipping through Playboy magazines or watching "adult" movies—pornography distorts your view of reality and is not okay for anyone, let alone teenagers. Internet porn is a far cry from the types of visual stimulation you grew up with.

In this situation, with this question, I can say it without apology: mom is right. This needs to be addressed in your home and you need to put some safeguards in place with your son so it doesn't happen any more. Start with X3watch (X3watch.com).

DD: In this case, I would say it's time for a sit-down with son and with dad, because the fact of the matter is that a lot of dads think it's "normal" for their sons to masturbate to porn because they're doing it themselves. I can understand the point of view that masturbating to pornography is "normal," because to a degree, that's true—as people, we seek to satisfy our urges.

The problem is that pornography, especially on the internet, is insidious. It's never a one-time thing, and the desire for it never stops. I've seen too many people start off on pornography and then ruin their lives through prostitution, affairs, and even criminal behavior.

In the case of the family mentioned in this question, it's time for an intervention of sorts. This mom, dad, and son need to sit down with a counselor, pastor, youth pastor, or some other sort of counseling professional and have a good, long talk or series of talks about what's right and what's wrong. Because this is clearly not right.

Another option would be for someone like this father and son to attend a XXXchurch "Porn and Pancakes" event (or, for women, "Porn and Pastries"). These are usually on a Saturday morning, hosted at a church, where men can come to hear about the true effects of porn, ask questions, and learn about things like accountability.

What's the problem with pornography?

Oddly enough, some people really do believe there is no problem with pornography, but we've seen otherwise through the ministry we do at XXXchurch. Though we mostly deal with adults who are addicted to using pornography, we've also noticed that most—if not all—of those adults were first exposed to porn as children. It can have a long, insidious impact on the mind of a child, an impact that will stay with them well into adulthood.

What kind of impact? First of all, porn damages their health emotionally and mentally, quickly desensitizing them to sex and often causing them to seek out ever more deviant imagery. Children are powered by curiosity, so it's only natural for them to dig deeper into such a titillating experience, seeking out more and more illicit content.

Also, just like in adults, porn blurs the lines between the fantasy portrayed on a screen and the real-life authenticity of sex. The actors in porn are just that—actors. They aren't really enjoying what they're doing; they're playing it up for the cameras. But it's difficult for kids to understand that, and so porn can warp their expectations for true sex when they finally begin to experience it. They'll want to act out what they've seen in porn.

Additionally, porn is all about the act of sex, depicting the participants as mere objects of gratification. There is no love, there is no commitment, there is no true intimacy represented in porn—there is only the physical now of two faceless bodies doing things that push the limits of the human body. As such, both boys and girls who view porn carry around feelings of shame and low self-worth, feeling like they can never measure up to the flawless performances they've seen in porn. Because that's all sex is to them: an act. A performance.

And finally, the images will stick with them far past their original exposure. What they see will stay somewhere in their mind for years, if not for their entire lifetime.

There really is no reason why anyone—let alone children—should be using pornography. Plain and simple.

How can I know if my child is using porn?

While you can't know for sure without actually catching your child in the act of using porn, there are a few subtle clues you can follow that might give away a possible porn problem.

Behaviorally, if you start to notice your child dressing more provocatively or incorporating more suggestive terminology into their vocabulary or with their friends, then they may be giving porn a try. You may also notice signs of premature sexual activity or an unhealthy curiosity about sex, sexuality, and all that pertains to those things.

There are also clues you can find on your family computer. Namely, if you notice a sudden surge in pop-up ads, spam emails, viruses, or find inappropriate content on the computer, then those are signs that your computer may have been used for porn. Other telltale warning signs are when the browser history has been cleared, if your child changes the screen quickly when you enter the room, or if they become defensive or secretive about their computer usage.

Another important thing to understand is that pornography is no longer just a "boys' issue"—girls now struggle with porn addiction, too. Is porn more prevalent among boys? Yes, absolutely. But girls aren't immune, and the rate of girls consuming porn is only increasing with its availability.

But ultimately, the best way to know is to keep an open dialogue with your child about the dangers of pornography and the temptations that lie within it. Be open with them about the topic, let them know that you're aware it exists, and don't let it be a dirty little secret in your house.

Oh, and if you're using it, you should probably stop. (You can get help to overcome your porn addiction through the resources at XXXchurch.com).

How do I keep my kids from accessing porn?

While you can't hover over your children every second of every day to prevent anything bad from ever happening to them—especially in the realm of porn exposure—you can take practical steps to help your kids stay away from it, and most of those practical steps have to do with getting a strategy for how you'll handle their access to the internet.

Obviously, we recommend X3watch, a software we created for this very purpose. There is a free version of X3watch available, which provides a frequent accountability report for any website visits that get flagged as being inappropriate. These reports can be emailed to up to two different accountability partners, who can then examine the reports and ask questions about those site visits to determine what was going on. Sometimes just knowing that someone else—especially a parent—will know that they've gone somewhere they shouldn't can prevent a child from making negative choices about where they spend their time online.

Beyond that simple accountability product, we also offer X3watch Premium, a beefed-up version of X3watch that also includes internet filtering, usage monitoring, customized URL blocking, and accountability. Plus, X3watch Premium works across multiple platforms, so you can take care of all your computers and mobile devices like smartphones and tablets with one account.

Now, there are some apps available for phones and tablets that offer what is known as "back-door" access to the internet, meaning that you can bypass some filters and get to the internet through the app rather than through the browser on your mobile device. You'll need to make sure you thoroughly test out these apps before you put these apps on your kids' mobile device(s), and you should always be the one with the password to install them. Don't let your kids manage their own apps.

My child said they saw porn at the neighbor's house. What do i do?

First things first, you need to talk with your son or

daughter. Then you need to talk with your neighbors and their kid and let them know what happened and what's going on. And you need to find out who showed them pornography—was it another child or was it an adult? Because if it was an adult, that person may have ulterior motives with your children and needs to be dealt with. Harshly. You might even need to call the authorities.

If they saw it because of a peer, that's another story. Personally, I wanted to talk to my kids about pornography before they saw pornography. I deal with this for a living, so we've actually already discussed this with both our kids—you may not have had similar discussions with yours.

What sort of language did I use when talking about pornography with my kids? I just told them that some people take photos of naked men and women to show off their private parts. And just like you don't want anyone touching your private areas, you don't want anyone seeing them, either, nor should you look at someone else's. They aren't for looking at.

If you see pornography going on in someone else's house and don't do anything about it, then there's a good chance it'll come into your house, too. It doesn't matter how good the neighbor's kids are, whether they're on honor roll at school or are winning major prizes in Sunday school at church—they could be dabbling in porn. They may have innocently typed something in to Google, but they accidentally misspelled it and now porn is just a click away.

So how do you deal with this? I'd recommend that you go to XXXchurch.com/parents and investigate those resources to find answers. Unlike this book, this website is continually updated as we add more and more parental resources to help parents like you tackle this topic.

DD: *Research has shown that most sexual activity among teenagers takes place immediately after school, during those couple of hours before mom or dad comes home from work when kids have the house to themselves.*

This also applies to viewing pornography.

This is why it pays to know what your kids are doing after school, who they're hanging out with, where they are... all those types of things. Don't think of it as being nosy or intrusive—look at it instead as being proactive and protective.

QUESTIONS ABOUT RELATIONSHIPS

What are your suggestions for dating?

My parents allowed me to date pretty early on, but that still presented a problem, because a lot of the girls I wanted to take out on a date weren't allowed to by their parents. In my case, a guy pursuing a girl, I honored whatever boundaries their parents had put in place for them. I did whatever they were allowed to do.

As far as dating goes for your kids, those rules are for you to set. We can't prescribe anything or espouse any one particular philosophy, because what's good for my house may not necessarily work in your house. The boundaries differ from house to house, even from kid to kid.

Personally, I think group settings are great, especially if your kids aren't old enough to drive themselves anywhere. By the time you're entrusting your kid with keys and a vehicle, you should be able to trust them with going out on a date.

Ages are going to be involved, too. Am I going to let my fourteen-year-old go out with a nineteen-year-old? No!

Another thing to keep in mind: where will they go? If

154

you're worried about what your kids would be doing out on a date, then make your house a place that attracts teenagers. Don't be awkward around them and don't try to be cool— just enjoy their company and get into their world and you'll find that your home will become a haven for them. It will be the kind of place where your kids want to hang out.

DD: My dating philosophy: If your daughter's date rolls up in a beat-up, 1976 van, stays in the driveway honking the horn, and rolls down the window to shout, "Come on, baby!" at her... it's probably a bad idea to let her go through with that particular evening.

If, on the other hand, you have an opportunity to meet your son or daughter's date for the evening, to talk with them and find out a little about where they're going and what they're doing, you'll feel a lot better. I know I always feel better when I get a few specifics, especially when it comes to my daughter. I'm not just going to send her out the door with any guy who wanders up.

What is an appropriate age for the first kiss?

You can control when your kids get their driver's

license. You can control the ways you allow them to date (even though they may go behind your back). However, there are some things you can't control, and this is one of them. In fact, I'd go so far as to say that you won't even know about their first kiss, at least not for awhile after it happens. Think about it: did your parents know about yours?

What you can control in this instance is the information you impart to them about dating and the opposite sex. You can give them good information about dating and the pursuit of relationships so that they can make good decisions, even about something as innocent-seeming as a first kiss. You can live your life as an example to them so that you aren't nervous or uncertain about this. You can give them as much knowledge beforehand as possible so they'll make wise decisions.

DD: *If you discover that your child is making out or you hear about some bout of kissing from someone other than your child, then you probably got into the game in the last quarter. You should've been there already, talking with your child, heading off any types of promiscuous behavior. Is kissing wrong? No, not necessarily. Are kids going to do it? Most likely. But it's important that you inform your son or daughter, maybe even when you have a sex talk, that kissing is a part of the feelings, emotions, and genuine care you feel for someone else. It's not something to take casually.*

What are good boundaries to give my children when it comes to hanging out with the opposite sex?

Guess what? You and your kids aren't friends—you're the parent; they're the child. As long as they live in your house, they live under your rules, and that definitely applies in this area. I see a "boundary" as a suggestion that you make to your kids, and when it comes to hanging out with members of the opposite sex, you don't need just boundaries, you need some guidelines and some actual rules.

These rules need to be rooted in common sense. For example: sure, son, you can have girls over to the house, but not in your bedroom, and not in any room with the door shut. See? It just makes sense.

There are some ways in which we never stop parenting, and this is one of those ways. As your kids get older, you'll have to talk through all the sorts of boundaries and rules you'll want to have for dating, physical contact, group dating, relationships… the list goes on. But whatever you decide, make sure it's your decision, not your kid's. Don't let your son or daughter call the shots.

I've seen this happen far, far too often, especially when it comes to the internet. Parents are clueless, kids set the rules, and trouble ensues. This same thing can happen in the area of relationships with the opposite sex, so you have to set rules and stick to them, even when your kids are young.

DD: *When my son was in high school, he dated a couple of girls, and he would bring them over to the house for dinner, for pizza and a movie, or whatever. You know the drill—the types of stuff that teenagers like to do. We always were glad that he felt comfortable enough bringing these young women home and making them a part of our world.*

But there was a time or two when he and his girlfriend would go down to the basement to watch a movie by themselves. Now, I understand the desire for a teenage boy to have a little privacy and to spend some time with his girl. And I was thankful that they were in our house watching a movie instead of watching each other in the backseat of his car in some parking lot.

However: my house, my rules. You can go down to the basement, but understand that the door stays open, and we'll come down any time we want. We still put a lot of trust in you not to put yourself in a compromising position, but we're going to put some boundaries in place to help you.

And yes, occasionally, I'd pop down there unannounced to grab a drink from the fridge, and I didn't care whether they found it annoying. I'm not their friend—I'm their dad. Plus, I was thirsty.

Should I expect my child to treat sex better than I did?

We all make mistakes, and some of us made a lot of mistakes in the area of sex when we were younger. So now the question is: are we going to let our kids make those same mistakes, or are we going to learn from them and teach our kids how to avoid the pitfalls we fell into?

Did you make a mistake by going down a wrong path? Tell your kids about it. Let them know why they shouldn't go down certain paths, and let them know you're speaking from experience and regret. That's the best way to prevent them from following in your footsteps.

There are certain things about my kids that resemble different qualities in me or my wife. My son has a cowlick in the same spot on his head that I do. My daughter's personality is very similar to my wife's. Some things our kids learn from environment while other things are genetic, and if you misused sex when you were younger, you should probably take extra precautions when it comes to your kids.

But ultimately, you can't impose behavior on them; you can just give them good information to help them make good decisions, and you can give them dire consequences if they make bad decisions. Unfortunately, when it comes to sex, the world can give them dire consequences as well: unexpected pregnancies, sexually transmitted diseases, broken hearts, physical pain... the list goes on.

Be honest about your past and hope your child learns lessons from your mistakes.

How do i tell my kids to wait in a way they will listen? Would it help if i talked to them about stds?

This is a concept that will drive many conversations in my household for years to come. It's not going to be, like, "Here's a purity ring. Don't have sex!" and be done. Instead, abstinence will be the foundational basis for most of our talks about sex, because it has such ramifications for other behavior, whether it's kissing, or making out, or petting, or oral sex.

If the goal is purity, then you have to consider why you're wanting to do those other things and whether you'll be able to stop once you've allowed them. If you're hoping to keep a pure heart, why are you trying to get as close to the line of "intercourse" as possible without crossing it?

People can refrain from having sex for multiple reasons, whether those are religious in nature, or moral, or emotional, or health-related. Any or all of those are good reasons to wait, so feel free to talk to your kids about STDs and the many reasons why they should avoid them. If you wait until you're married, then only have sex with your spouse, you'll probably never get an STD and will never have to get tested. AIDS will not be a fear for you.

These are the types of things I want my kids to think about. It's not about white-knuckling your way through temptation or pushing things as far as you can go and hoping you can make it through unscathed and free of disease. It's about approaching sex with an attitude of purity, respect, and reverence.

DD: In our house, we used a metaphor of snow skiing. When you go skiing, you go to the top of the hill and start down it. But when you're halfway down, you aren't going to stop and say, "I'm done." No way! You're going to ski as far as you can, all the way to the bottom.

In the same way, sexual activity is a ski slope, and once you start down it, it's tough to stop. You may have good intentions going into it, but temptation takes over and makes it all the more difficult to stop once you've started down the slope. So it's best not to start down the hill in the first place. Be careful about the situations you let yourself get into.

As for STDs, I only have this to say: we teach our kids that Christopher Columbus discovered the Americas, but we tend to leave out the fact that he died of syphilis.

Well, he was an explorer.

My daughter thinks she's in love with her boyfriend and wants to give up her virginity. What do i do?

You'll likely hear more about this from your daughters than you will from your sons. Boys tend to think "sex" while girls tend to think "love." Guys will use love to get sex while girls will use sex to get love, even though in both instances, that particular "love" is of a cheap sort.

In a case like this, you have to remind your daughter that this guy probably doesn't love her. If he did, he would respect her enough to wait for her. It's tough, especially when her adolescent hormones are telling her otherwise and that the emotions she's feeling are true love.

The best you can do is try to help her get level-headed once more and see things for what they really are. Let her know that the chances of having a lasting relationship with your high school sweetheart are very slim, and so does she really want to give away her virginity like that? It isn't something you should give away to just anyone—it's meant for the person you're going to spend the rest of your life with.

DD: Parents, we can tell our daughters a million times a day never to trust her emotions, and we still wouldn't be saying it enough. The bottom line to this is that oftentimes a young girl makes decisions based on what her emotions tell her.

My daughter has friends who can fall in love with three

or four different guys a week, based on how a certain boy looked at them or talked to them or treated them. Girls are often too ready to make commitments based on emotion alone. We have to keep this in mind as we're talking to them about sex, and especially virginity.

What if my child is already having sex?

If your child is already doing it, and you're aware of it, and it's just an open thing, then you as a parent have to make some changes so they don't keep having those opportunities. Don't be convinced that this type of behavior is okay, and don't keep allowing it to happen under your roof.

Sure, there's a good chance they're having sex behind your back, and that if you confront them about it, they'll still keep doing it. That's their choice, and sex is a powerful drug. You could be doing everything right, you could have followed every principle we've given you in this book, and it can still happen. Don't beat yourself up about it—it's ultimately your child's decision on whether or not they're going to do it.

Here's a huge thing to keep in mind: once kids start having sex, it's going to be tough to stop, because it's too easy for them to think, "Well, I already lost my virginity, so what's the big deal?" But you can encourage your kids that they can stop and do what they set their minds to.

DD: *My family is friends with a young man who became sexually active when he was in the seventh or eighth grade. He is now a junior in high school and has fathered two children. His sexual past is littered with heartbreak and emotional trauma, both in himself and in the girls he's had sex with. He never had a father figure in his life to sit down and tell him that what he's doing is not right. Who knows what would've happened if someone had taken the time to explain to him the power of sex and the dangers of going down the road he's been going down?*

Now is the time to sit down with your child and talk to them about these things. To take precautions and every step you can to guide your children toward a pure heart and mind.

| QUESTIONS ABOUT CULTURE |

How do we talk about issues like homosexuality, and at what age?

We'll have another question a little later in the book where we'll address this from a teenage perspective, but for now, let's talk about ways you can discuss this with younger kids.

For starters, address it as it is introduced. This is one area where you do not have to take initiative and strike up the conversation with your younger kids. There's really no need to bring it up unless your kids are somehow exposed to it, whether it be through the media or their peers or some well-intentioned adult. In these days where politics are widely discussed on radio and television and the phrase "gay marriage" is thrown around like a Frisbee at a family picnic, it's very easy for your child to be exposed innocently to the topic.

If they do wind up hearing about homosexuality, instead of dreading it, embrace it instead as another opportunity to talk to your kids about sex. You can say something like, "You have a mom and a dad, but there are some kids who have two moms or two dads." And that's pretty much all you really need to say at this point.

Avoiding it further isn't going to help things. It's just going to create weirdness, and where kids sense weirdness, they get uncomfortable and clam up.

The last weekend of June is typically celebrated in the homosexual community as a sort of "gay pride" weekend. I was speaking in Seattle, Washington with my young children during one of these weekends. I hadn't planned it; it just turned out that way. One evening, while we were walking down the sidewalk in downtown on our way to meet some friends for dinner, we took a turn and stumbled onto a gay pride parade.

I don't know if you've ever seen a gay pride parade, but they generally don't just represent homosexuality in and of itself—most participants showcase an extreme version of the gay lifestyle. There was kissing, and revealing costumes, and signs with not-kid-friendly slogans… the whole nine yards.

In that moment, I had a choice. I could either ignore what was going on and let my kids be confused, or I could take the opportunity to provide a cursory explanation. So I said, "In our country, people have a choice to do this, and that's what these people are doing," and left it at that. My kids didn't really have any questions beyond that, but if they had, I would've done my best to answer them honestly.

But to cover their eyes and speed up in an attempt to pretend homosexuality doesn't exist would've been detrimental. Do I want to be at a gay pride weekend with my kids? Not usually. But since I was put in that situation, I might as well tackle the topic and move on.

DD: *Once more, this goes back to that idea of having an ongoing conversation about sex. There are so many aspects of sex, from heterosexuality to homosexuality to trans-sexuality that your child is going to see, notice, or pick up on through life, media, the internet, wherever. Any time they do, it's an open door to talk to your kids about that particular facet of sexuality.*

In an ironic twist of fate, at the same time Craig was marching his kids through a gay pride parade in downtown Seattle, I was with my daughter in Chicago, and we had stumbled onto the same thing. Now, she's a lot older than Craig's kids, so I was able to use this as a springboard to an in-depth discussion not just about homosexuality in general but the way many in the homosexual community choose to live and represent themselves to the world. It was a great time to share our thoughts and feelings, and we were able to do that because we've laid a foundation from the time she was young where talking about sex is normal and healthy.

My kid has gay friends. What do i say about that?

We talked a little bit about how you handle this with

your younger kids—once your kids are old enough to know what homosexuality is and even to know someone who is homosexual, it's time to talk more about it. For all you know, your kids could even be dealing with homosexual feelings themselves.

Once they're in high school, your kids are going to hear words like "gay," "lesbian," "bisexual," "transgender," and all sort of other definitions of sexuality. They'll also run across a few friends who claim to be one or more of those things. And so, once more, you owe it to your kids to talk these things through. You can't be scared of these conversations.

As far as how you should treat your kids' friends who identify themselves sexually as gay: just treat them like you would treat any other kid. Your job as a parent is to lead by example and show love to everyone, no matter who they are, and that includes every single person who comes into your house.

DD: This is becoming more and more prevalent in our society, and we are seeing more outspoken gay and lesbian teenagers than we ever have before. This isn't going away and it's not something you can ignore. You may not agree with the lifestyle, but it's still your job to love them and to show them kindness and respect. This is not something to snicker about or to denigrate.

My daughter is reading romance-type novels. Is this okay?

In the same way that you should monitor the movies and TV shows your kids watch or the internet sites they visit, you should definitely check out the books they're reading. Much of what passes for literature today is questionable, and girls tend to get more emotionally attached than guys do. Guys want to look at pictures or video to find stimulation while girls tend to ground their fantasies in emotion and story.

It never hurts to take precautions and know what your girl might be reading. It might take awhile, but read the books ahead of time so you know exactly what sort of content they're going to taking in. Not only does this keep you clued in on what they're reading, but it also gives you the opportunity to discuss it with them.

Also, make sure what your kids are reading is age-appropriate. Some parents are just elated to see their child reading a book instead of sucking up video games, but if your ten-year-old is reading Twilight… that's probably not okay. Make sure what they're reading is something they can handle both emotionally and intellectually. There will come a time for them to read something geared toward older ages, but they need to have the emotional foundation to handle it.

DD: This is an epidemic that extends far beyond teenage girls, all the way up to middle-aged women and even women older than that, where they can wind up spending more time with these idealized, unrealistic stories rather than engaging in real life. It portrays a false reality of what most relationships are like and can lead to frustration in regular life.

Also, those character names can get ridiculous. Have you ever met an emotionally wounded cowboy named Colt Stronghand or Dirk Trueblood?

Should I place any media restrictions on my kids?

The answer to this question is: absolutely yes.

So then you have to decide: where do you draw those restrictive lines?

We can't answer that question for you, but we can help you have some guidelines. First, understand that your kids are probably smarter and more sophisticated than you might initially think. They get it. They know what's going on, even if they can't always articulate it. They don't have a whole lot of critical thinking skills yet—that doesn't really come into play until adulthood—but they do tend to be pretty savvy.

So it's up to you to help them navigate the culture and the world. You don't want to be too permissive, because you might wind up letting your kids exposed to ideas, concepts, or sights they aren't emotionally ready to handle, but on the other hand, you don't want to be so restrictive that you don't teach your kids to develop good judgment and the ability to choose to stop watching something they know probably isn't good for them.

Ultimately it's a balancing act of paying attention to your kids' behavior and reactions to things while simultaneously doing what you can to guard their hearts. And remember: they take their cues from you, so if you freak out about something, they're going to freak out about it, too. So play it smart, play it cool, play it safe, and trust your gut.

I'm in the dark about popular video games. What can you tell me?

Among many kids, video games carry more cultural currency than popular movies or television shows. Release dates are anticipated and celebrated, and new games are played in community marathon sessions. For a large subset of the population, nothing brings those members together than bonding over a new video game.

Gaming today spans a large spectrum of content, playability, and platforms, from puzzle games to "first-person shooters" to the kinds of games that create immersive worlds that players can explore at their own leisure. And these games exist in specific platforms like the X-Box or Playstation, online gaming that only require a computer and an internet connection, or mobile games designed specifically for mobile devices.

It would be impossible to discuss in this book all that you need to know about gaming, especially because much of what's popular in gaming changes so quickly (that's partially why we created iParent.TV!). But there are a few general observations we can make that might help you as you guide your video-game-interested children through that world.

First, think of games as much in the same way as you would movies or television shows: there are different levels of content intended for different levels of maturity. Some games are perfectly acceptable for just about anyone; some are so saturated with sex and violence that they're barely acceptable even for the most hard-hearted adult; most are somewhere in between.

The Entertainment Software Rating Board rates games for parents, working generally in the same way as the Motion Picture Association of America's rating system; however, just like that system, it's not very reliable for across-the-board adoption. However, the ESRB's guidelines are a handy barometer and starting place for parents as they first consider allowing a specific game.

But, just like the rest of the media you allow your children to use, you should set your own standards and trust your instincts. And when it comes to this stuff, nothing can beat sharing game time with your kids! Play along with them and don't be afraid to push "pause" and discuss questionable things within what you're playing or to talk about any other aspects of life that gaming can bring up, including the power of perseverance and the self-control you develop by limiting the amount of time spent playing the game. Gaming can be a terrific bonding experience if you do it right.

Are online video games better or worse than platform games?

Content wise, online games are, by and large, roughly the same as video games that are played offline. But while all forms of media have some inherent dangers, online video games have a few that are exclusive to the online aspect of them.

In addition to the violent content often found in video games, some online games feature borderline pornographic images—and a few even have porn embedded into them as part of the experience, melding the gaming industry with the porn industry to generate income and website visits to popular porn sites.

One of the main features of the online game is the multiplayer aspect, where players from different locations can meet up within the game and play either against one another or together as a team. As you can imagine, this creates a virtual playground for online predators, who use the game to connect with kids, share experiences with them, build trust and camaraderie, and then parlay that trust into an offline meet-up.

The multiplayer facet of online gaming also makes a great attraction for cyberbullies to torment perceived weaker kids within the game, often using adult language in the process.

And then, just like with most online usage, there is the problem of privacy and identity theft—something to consider whenever you let your kids loose on the internet, but especially in online gaming. Plus, there is the addictive aspect of gaming to contend with, where kids can spend hours within the gaming environment and begin to blur the lines between their virtual world and the real one around them.

My twelve-year-old met someone online. Is this okay?

Absolutely not. I'll go even farther: if your kids are on the computer and are able to interact with complete strangers, there is something wrong with your parenting. You've given them access to a computer, an iPad, a smartphone, an iPod Touch, or some other piece of technology that they clearly do not know how to operate. Yes, they know how to use it to get around on the internet, but they don't know what they're doing. They don't know the dangers they're putting themselves in or what is actually taking place.

Don't take the internet at face value. There are too many people out there who are putting forth a version of themselves that isn't true, that isn't reality. There are some truly frightening people out there just looking for kids. These people have motives that are downright criminal and evil. If your kids don't know who they're talking to online, they shouldn't be talking to them at all.

DD: For me, this is a warning sign that your twelve-year-old, whether female or male, may not be getting enough attention at home. Otherwise, why are they out looking for companionship on the internet? They're looking for ways to share thoughts, feelings, dreams, passions in life... they want someone to hear what they have to say. Unfortunately, there are unsavory, malicious people on the internet who are all too eager to listen.

They'll start up a conversation and listen, but it never stops there. These things, when allowed to go on, almost inevitably lead to sexual activity, usually by an online predator. This is nothing to joke about—if you see this happening with your child, step in and stop it.

QUESTIONS ABOUT THE INTERNET

What sorts of guidelines should i set
for my kids' online activities?

Keeping your kids safe online is practically a full-time job for today's parent, but we do have some general ideas on the kinds of guidelines you should set for them as they learn to navigate the online minefield.

First, as we've hopefully hammered home throughout this book—keep the conversations going with them. You don't need to badger them every time they open a new browser tab, but it's very good to check in with them every now and then to see how they're doing, to find out where they're going, and to determine whether they've made some missteps along the way. By taking the initiative to keep the lines of communication open with your kids, you embolden them to come to you with questions or concerns.

By keeping your door open like that, you'll be more likely to feel safe to your kids if they ever feel scared, threatened, or uncomfortable about something that happened online, whether it's a site they visit or someone who communicates with them. There's no need to overreact and there's certainly no need to blame your child for anything, because you want them to feel secure in coming to you. Now's the time to build a strong foundation for future communication.

Also, don't let your kids wonder about where you stand on where they can go—make a physical list of rules for their internet consumption. This list can include anything from a restricted list of sites they can visit, to time limits on how long any one session can last, to whom they communicate with while they're using the web. Put it in writing so they know exactly what they can and can't do, and don't be afraid to update or revise the list as new technologies come online.

This one's a no-brainer for us, but X3watch is a must. The whole point of X3watch is to have an online strategy and to help guard your kids' hearts as they use the web; investigate installing it on all your devices to help you supervise and monitor the ways your kids use them.

And finally, always remind your kids of the golden rule: treat others however they would want to be treated—if they wouldn't say it directly to someone while everyone's parents were watching, then they shouldn't say it online (or in a text message or through social media, either!).

How restrictive should i be about social media?

Social media is growing into a giant, lumbering beast that is increasingly taking up more and more of our cultural landscape. In some ways it seems unavoidable, like a foregone conclusion that you have to sign your kids up for. But we don't think so.

Do what you feel is right when it comes to social media and your kids—because in the long run, they really aren't missing much if they aren't interacting with others through social media. As I wrote earlier—I would much rather my kids focus on their face-to-face, real relationships with actual people than on tinkering with some online profile or portal.

That said, if you do choose to let your kids use social media, here are some thoughts we recommend you consider when setting your child up for any social networking.

Don't let your child on any site or network that you aren't already a member of. If they want to join Facebook, you need to be on Facebook. You need to know the ins and outs of Facebook. You need to see how your kids' friends use Facebook. You get the idea. Don't throw your son or daughter onto a social networking site you know nothing about—take the time to investigate it and see if it's a place where your kids can be safe.

Also, you should definitely have continuous conversations with your kids about their online behavior. There's something about being online, especially in a social media context, that creates a disconnect in the way we act in the real world and the persona we use online. So talk with your children about behaving appropriately, thinking through anything they post before they post it. There are no take-backs online—even if you delete something after you post it, the fingerprints of it can still be there. Especially now that so much social is happening on mobile devices, where screenshots can be gotten in a couple of seconds and sent around for eternity.

Should you allow your kids into the world of social media, it's important that you don't let them on alone. Know what they're doing and who they're talking to. At this point in their lives, don't let them befriend people on social media that they don't already know in real life—they don't need to have "online-only" friends. And don't forget to check their privacy settings frequently to make sure they're set to the highest level.

Teenagers also tend to find creative ways to use social media and technology to explore their sexuality, so have a frank discussion with your teenager about the dangers of online sex (and real-world sex, too!), especially the fakeness of it. Unfortunately, the world has far too many predators who want to seek out and groom potential victims, not to mention the sexualized world of adolescents, where peers pressure one another to send provocative images and/or text. If someone is pressuring your child to do so, they aren't a friend and need to be blocked.

Social media can be beneficial in some respects, but it also has a lot of pitfalls you'll have to help your son or daughter learn to avoid. Help them navigate the social media landscape carefully.

Should i be concerned about cyber-bullying?

Bullying is just part of the human experience, especially in the world of childhood as kids are rapidly discovering who they really are and attempt to assert their place in the world. But while bullying exists, that doesn't mean we have to necessarily endorse it or accept it. Especially when it comes barging into the safe realm of our homes through technology.

We're talking about cyber-bullying, which is just regular old harassment happening through network-connected devices. What does cyber-bullying entail? It can be anything like rumors, name-calling, or images or videos posted through social media or any other online forum where others can see them. Cyber-bullies also occasionally impersonate someone or create a group page intended to shame a particular individual or make them feel left out.

So what can you do about cyber-bullying? It all starts, just like everything else, with a conversation with your kids. Talk with them about bullying and what it looks like, discovering whether they've ever been cyber-bullied or whether they've ever intentionally or unintentionally bullied someone. You can ask questions like:

- What kinds of information do you consider to be safe? What about information that is unsafe?

- What are your privacy settings right now?

- Say you have a friend you know is being bullied. Would you help them? What specific ways would you go about doing that?

- Have you ever been bullied? How did it make you feel?

183

These kinds of questions are great conversation starters and, though they might feel a little awkward at first, they're essential to guiding your kids through this particular aspect of modern-day adolescence.

Be sure your kids know that one of the key aspects to maintaining online integrity is understanding the ramifications of the things they say or post. Passive-aggression is an internet staple, but it's stupid. If they wouldn't say it to someone in person, in front of authority figures, then they shouldn't say it online (and that goes for you, too, mom or dad!).

If someone has been cyber-bullying your child, there are some steps you can take. First, don't overreact or escalate the situation. Tell your child to cut off contact with the bully immediately, blocking whatever avenues that bully might have to continue harassing them. But keep a copy of the evidence, first! You might need those messages if the behavior escalates and you have to get the authorities involved. Bullies generally act out because they like the reaction they get from those they bully—if their victims don't react, they'll likely move on.

If your child knows someone who is being bullied or sees bullying in action, encourage them to help stop it.

Don't forward bullying content to others. If the bullying is happening through social media, report the bully to that site's moderators, and don't hesitate to schedule a conversation with that bully's parents if the situation requires it.

Think your child might be the victim of bullying? It's possible—be on the lookout for some of the typical behavioral changes that come about as a result of bullying, like a reluctance to go to school, or to get online or use their mobile device. If your child suddenly changes their behavior, something is influencing that; it may well be cyber-bullying.

| QUESTIONS ABOUT SEXTING |

What is 'sexting,' anyway? I keep hearing about it but don't know what it is.

Take a kid with raging hormones and a limited capacity for critical thinking, then give them a mobile computer with a camera and a connection to the outside world, and then top it all off with creative imagination.

That's sexting.

More specifically, sexting is when people use their mobile device to create and exchange provocative, nude, semi-nude, or sexual images of themselves, or provocative text.

You can see where this is going.

Sexting isn't quite the worrisome epidemic that we once thought it was, but it is still very much present in some parts of the world of people today, and so it is something you should make sure your kids are aware of. Talk with them about sexting, setting clear boundaries about what is appropriate and inappropriate use of modern technology.

Behaviors like sexting can have serious emotional consequences, especially since images can be captured and shared instantaneously over the internet. Once your child sends anything out into the digital world, it is out of their hands and can be there forever. It's crucial that they understand this, knowing that what they share will likely not stay with the person they are sharing it with.

You may want to consider setting limits on the types of messages your child can send and receive on their phone; check with your mobile provider to see what they offer in the ways of parental controls.

And if you find out your child has sent or received a sext, remain calm. Overreacting or escalating isn't going to help.

Instead, talk through the behavior with your child, seeking outside counseling help if necessary or, if applicable, the proper authorities.

I saw some inappropriate text messages on my child's phone. How should i confront them?

DD: First off, congratulations on doing the right thing. If you're paying for the phone or the phone service and your child is living in your house, then you have every right to look at their phone anytime you want. A phone is not a right; it's not even a privilege. For a teenager, a phone is a luxury item.

A friend of mine was out to dinner with his family not too long ago and began to question some of his son's texting habits. One thing led to another and my friend demanded to see his son's phone immediately. Knowing this is just part of the deal, the son handed over the phone and there they were, in Applebee's, my friend scrolling through his son's text messages over dinner.

I think that's fantastic. Is it an invasion of privacy? No, absolutely not. It's part of the responsibility of having a phone.

We had the same thing happen in our house once. After my son had gone to bed one night, my wife and I looked through his text messages and found some stuff that was definitely inappropriate. We actually went so far as to wake him up so we could confront him about it, which let him know how important it was to us. He admitted to his actions and we were able to take care of the situation and defuse the bomb right then and there.

How your kids use their phones could wind up being serious business. This may not hold true for your state, but I live in Indiana, where kids can get into big trouble for what they send with their phones. If one kid under the age of 18 takes a picture of their genitalia with their phone and then sends it to another kid under the age of 18, both of them have just broken the law and have participated in child pornography.

Know what's on your kid's phone. If they're doing more with it than they should, confiscate it. Eventually, they'll figure out how to breathe without one.

What kinds of legal problems can sexting cause?

Sexting can have serious legal problems, as we've already seen as police have begun investing this use of technology among young people. Consequences have ranged from suspension from school to felony charges for the creation and distribution of child pornography. Kids are doing jail time for sexting, and they will forever have to be registered as sex offenders.

This is one area of the law with little room for leniency. If your child receives a sexually suggestive image of one of their peers (who is under the age of 18) and they keep it, they could be charged with possession of child pornography. Pure and simple. If they're under the age of 18 and they send a sexual image of themselves, they could be charged with creation and distribution of child pornography.

In the eyes of the law, sexting is no joke, and it is not harmless fun. It is a serious crime with serious consequences. Please make sure your child understands the severity of sexting and steers far clear of it.

Conclusion

When it's all said and done, all parents want to see their children grow into responsible, well-adjusted, mentally healthy adults.

But they won't get there on their own. After all, you are not raising a child—you're raising a future adult, and there are going to be some tough times between birth and adulthood.

We hope you take this message to heart when talking to your kids about any of these important touchy subjects. Let them know how much you love them, how deeply you care for them, and that you are having this dialogue because you want to see them succeed in life.

Don't wait. Your kids might hear about these things from their friends, from their siblings, from other family, from television, from movies, from a book, from the internet... but none of those sources loves your children as much as you do.

Let them hear about it from you.

Let them keep hearing about it from you.

When they're grown, they'll thank you for it.

You can do it.

Trust us.

—Craig and David

BRING US OUT FOR AN EVENT

CRAIG
GROSS

DAVID
DEAN

CONTACT

(626) 628-3387 -or- Michelle@XXXChurch.com
Still have questions?
Email Craig@XXXChurch.com

iparent.tv

Parenting is tough...
Tech doesn't have to be

www.iparent.tv

ONLINE ACCOUNTABILITY FOR EVERY DEVICE

www.x3watch.com

27278955R00116

Made in the USA
San Bernardino, CA
11 December 2015